Library of Victorian Culture

Late Victorian Decor

from

Eastlake's Gothic to Cook's House Beautiful

Edited by Hugh Guthrie

AMERICAN LIFE FOUNDATION

1968

Library of Victorian Culture

How to Make and Restore Objets D'Art.

New Light on Old Lamps.

Victorian Silver: Holloware and Flatware.

Downing's Cottage Residences,
Landscapes Gardening, Rural Architecture.

Victorian Social & Political Satire.

Victorian Art Pottery.

Children's Picture Books,
Yesterday & Today.

Currier & Ives Victorian Battle Scenes.

Victorian Furnishings & Eastlake Design.

Victorian Poster Art.

Together with ten other promised titles, as suggested
by the American Life Foundation's Study Institute.

A NOTE FROM THE PUBLISHER

Charles Eastlake's *Hints on Household Taste* (London, 1868) and Clarence Cook's *House Beautiful* (N.Y., 1877) did so much to redress the interiors of Late Victorian homes that we debated reproducing separately the entirety of both volumes. The result would have been two books that were costly, filled with redundancies, and dulled by superfluous comments irrelevant to current collector interests and decorative trends. Instead, we have exerpted the most important passages from each. We hope this new edition of these classics which are practically unobtainable on the rare book market will find new usefulness amongst students, dealers, and decorators wanting to recapture an old mode just coming back into new vogue.

Following, we list the chapter headings of these two books along with the number of pages devoted by each topic which indicate the author's relative interest in his subject. Eastlake, *Hints on Household Taste* (forming Part I of this book): Introduction (13), Street Architecture (22), Entrance Hall (27), Dining Room (30), Floor & Wall Coverings (19), Library (27), Drawing Room (24), Wall Furniture (15), Bedroom (16), Crockery (20), Table Glass (15), Dress & Jewelry (21), Plate & Cutlery (13). Cook, *House Beautiful* (forming Part II of this book): The Entrance (21), Living Room (152), Dining Room (168), Bedroom (48), Words Here & There (3).

Besides Eastlake and Cook, other arbiters of Late Victorian taste for decoration and furniture have been considered in Part III of this book. They are English architects B. E. Smith and R. W. Edis, American architect H. H. Richardson, American art critic Harriet P. Spofford (her *Art Decoration Applied to Furniture,* N.Y., 1877, will soon appear as a separate volume in our Library of Victorian Culture).

EDITOR'S INTRODUCTION

In spite of being written exactly one hundred years ago, *Hints on Household Taste* by Charles Lock Eastlake (1836-1906) has lost none of its original impact for it is like our own age—violent and sarcastic. His criticisms are those of a highly concerned male—direct, straight-forward, and practical; another individual raising his cry against the maelstrom of Victorian female taste. It is on this note that he introduces his book. From here he vigorously condemns everything he surveys, from jewelery to crockery, door-mats to wall-coverings, picture frames to over-mantles. He particularly despises the sort of furnishings that were shown at the Crystal Palace Exhibition of 1851 and produced in great abundance afterwards—in other words, things made during the hey-day of his uncle, Sir Charles Eastlake, President of the Royal Academy. With equal fury, of course, Eastlake promotes his own rigorous aesthetic.

Now, of course the dubious reward of this stout-hearted campaign to reform the fussiness of mid-Victorian interiors was having a decorative style named after him. Unfortunately, Eastlake Golden Oak Gothic in the United States has been like the tail on the donkey: pinned onto the worst Late Victorian horrors that Grand Rapids stamped out and glued together during the 70's and 80's. The result of this unjust association has been the idea that Eastlake is an entity that is both deadly and dead-end. It is not. Until you understand the basic principles behind Eastlake design you will continue to think of it in this fashion. Eastlake (who was a devoted disciple of William Morris and John Ruskin) followed the principles of the Arts and Crafts Movement: "honest use of materials and frank expression of structure." His adherence to these principles place him in direct ancestral lineage to latter-day Arts and Crafts designers like Gustav Stickley and his 'Mission' furniture, Frank Lloyd Wright and his Prairie School, even present-day Scandinavian Modern. Thus Eastlake lives on and still is a vital force in decorative design.

Arts and Crafts principles motivate Eastlake's love of sturdy, simple, straight-line, functional, unvarnished, four-square furniture in which wood is used as wood, in which natural graining of the wood, essential hardware, and basic structural pegging (no glue!) serve as the only decoration, in which upholstery is kept to a minimum, and in which the virtues of Gothic English vernacular furnishings are exemplified. Eastlake also felt that all furnishings should be part of a total design concept rather than a mad-cap assortment of 'tasteful' novelties. It is this idea that Frank Lloyd Wright carried to an extreme when he screwed dining chairs to the floor, made surprise inspections of his thistle arrangements, and installed as much built-in furniture as his indulgent patrons could tolerate.

The Arts and and Crafts Movement was followed mainly by men who were at ill-ease in a female house; so it is predictable that Charles Eastlake shunned the taste of women, sycophant decorators, milliners, and upholsterers. He also disparaged the French Louis styles, curves, excess padding, varnished surfaces, mitred picture frames, florid carpets, and all other arbiters of taste, fashion, and novelty.

Eastlake's *Hints on Household Taste* (forming Part I of this book) had an enormous influence here as well as in England. As Russell Lynes points out in his *Tastemakers* (here exerpted courtesy the author and publisher), the ardent American champions of the Eastlake aesthetic included a Boston Brahmin, an unbalanced female enthusiast, and a shopkeeper who saw money in the new vogue. Charles Perkins, the leader of the Boston art establishment, wrote "in America we borrow second-hand and do not pretend to have a national taste, the patterns of our manufactures are taken from all parts of the world; we do nothing really original but trotting wagons and wooden clocks." His remedy was to read Eastlake and "go forth to sin no more." What Mrs. Sherwood lacked in Perkins' "cultivated artificiality" was made up by uncritical enthusiasm. "We must have beauty around us to make us good," she wrote, "the soothing influence of an Eastlake bookcase on an irritated husband has never been sufficiently calculated." Shopkeeper C. W. Elliot was said to have "sets of beautiful and artistic furniture, a passion for sincere bric-a-brac, and wallpaper which will not offend the principles of William Morris." Actually, the most successful of all American interpreters of Eastlake during the '70's was Mrs. Rodman. In her *How to Furnish a Home* she wrote, "a pine table is a proper thing, but one that pretends to be black walnut is an abomination." This leads us to that arbiter of interior furnishings for the next two decades, *The House Beautiful*.

In counter-distinction to Eastlake is Clarence Cook, a contemporary American critic of American fine and decorative arts for *Scribner's Monthly*. Although Cook lacks Eastlake's directness and pungency of expression, clearly, he is influenced by him. He differs from Eastlake in his tendency to advocate a more costly and mixed-style decor. This is to be expected, as the United States was more addicted to the historic styles than England. Properly, he may be credited with coining the phrase 'The House Beautiful.' Excerpts from his book of that title abound in woodcuts picturing commercially-made pieces which he thought appropriate to his own New York Brownstone. Part II of this book is rather sketchy since Cook, unlike Eastlake, created no unique style of his own. His main importance is his promotion of 'Art' furniture and 'Art' furnishings, an idea that gathered force during the 80's and 90's and culminated in turn-of-the-century Art Nouveau.

An important unheeded point, made by both Eastlake and Cook, is that tasteful home decorations need not be expensive. One reader of their pages wrote: "We are tired of spending money just to catch the new mode. Besides, you told us in the beginning you were going to show us how to make our houses pretty on next to nothing." Cook pointed out "nothing worth having comes without expenditure of time and money, but many of the best things in house furnishings are those that cost the least." And Eastlake said, "Taste requires to be popularized to render it profitable to the trade; but whether it will ever become popular while people can buy more showy articles at a less price, is the question."

Hugh Guthrie

Part I

Hints on Household Taste

in Furniture, Upholstery and Other Details

by Charles L. Eastlake

London 1868

————————

AUTHOR'S PREFACE

Some time ago a little essay of mine on "The Fashion of Furniture" led to my being invited to write for *The Queen* a series of articles on the same subject. These, combined with others recently contributed to the *London Review* have formed material for the present volume. I could have wished for more cuts (drawn on wood by myself or roughly sketched for the photographic process) to illustrate the character of design which I advocate; but this was impossible without materially increasing the cost of my book and thus interfering with its object: to suggest some fixed principles of popular taste for those not accustomed to heed them.

For although style and design in art manufacture has been treated in a technical, a metaphysical, and a historical fashion before, I am not aware it is treated in a manner sufficiently practical to insure public attention. My *Hints on Household Taste* is published to supply this deficiency. For without such public support, as every artist knows, all attempts in the direction of aesthetical reform are hopeless.

Choose, then, high aim in pictorial art.   People get into a
way of calling things 'quaint' and 'peculiar' which happen
to differ from the conventional ugliness of the modern
drawing-room.   When crinoline, for instance, was in the
height of its fashion, any young lady who had the courage
to appear without it would have been called 'a fright' in
regard to her toilet, without reference to the patent fact that
the folds of her dress thus fell much more gracefully than
when stretched over the steel hoop which, we are rejoiced
to see, is once more to be trundled into oblivion.   Now, if
we reflect on the baneful influence which this wretched
invention must have had for the last ten years on the tastes
of the rising generation; how children must have grown
up in the belief that it actually lent a sort of charm to the
skirts of their mothers' dresses, we shall begin to feel by
how much the less than ourselves little misses who are still
in their teens will be capable of appreciating the Venus of
Milo or the drapery of any other antique statue.   In the
same way, if we contemplate with satisfaction—nay, if we
even tolerate the extravagant and graceless appointments
of the modern boudoir, let us not be surprised that we find
it mirrored on the modern canvas.   The most natural
instinct of the painter's mind is, after all, to depict life as
he finds it; and in all the best ages of art this was practically done, even by those whose aim tended towards the
ideal.   Phidias, Raphael, and, if we may place their names

together, Hogarth, here met on common ground. We can hardly hope, then, in our own time, to sustain anything like a real and national interest in art while we tamely submit to the ugliness of modern manufacture. We cannot consistently have one taste for the drawing-room and another for the studio ; but, perhaps, the best discipline which could be devised for the latter would be initiated by a thorough reform of the first.

The faculty of distinguishing good from bad design in the familiar objects of domestic life is a faculty which most educated people—and women especially—conceive that they possess. How it has been acquired, few would be able to explain. The general impression seems to be that it is the peculiar inheritance of gentle blood, and independent of all training ; that while a young lady is devoting at school, or under a governess, so many hours a day to music, so many to languages, and so many to general science, she is all this time unconsciously forming that sense of the beautiful, which we call taste—that this sense, once developed, will enable her, unassisted by special study or experience, not only to appreciate the charms of nature in every aspect, but to form a correct estimate of the merits of art manufacture. That this impression has gained ground so far as to amount to positive conviction, may be inferred from the fact that there is no single point on which well-bred women are more jealous of disparagement than this.   We may condemn a lady's opinion on politics—criticize her handwriting—correct her pronunciation of Latin, and run down her favourite author with a chance of escaping displeasure.   But if we venture to question her taste—in the most ordinary sense of the word, we are sure to offend.   It is, however, a lamentable fact that this very quality is commonly deficient, not only among the generally ignorant, but also among the most educated classes in this country.   How should it be otherwise?   Even the simplest and most elementary principles of decorative art form no part of early instruction, and the majority of the public, being left completely uninformed of them, is content to be guided by a few people who are themselves not only uninformed but misinformed on the subject.   It is scarcely too much to say that ninety-nine out of every hundred English gentlewomen who have the credit of dressing well depend entirely upon their milliners for advice as to what they may, and what they may not, wear. The latest novelty from Paris is recommended—not because it has any special merit on the score of artistic beauty, but simply because it is a novelty.   Of course, it would be useless to urge, in answer to this, that a certain form of dress, once accepted as good, must always be good, or to deny that a particular combination of colours, recognised as harmonious, can become discordant, simply because it does not appear in the pages of *Le Follet*.   Unfortunately

the world of fashion is so constituted that people who move
in it are obliged to conform more or less to its rules; and
as no lady likes to make herself conspicuous by her attire,
she may reasonably abstain from wearing what has been
long out of date.   But there is a limit to all things; and
the capricious tyranny which insists on a monthly change
of dress ought to be firmly resisted by women who are too
sensible to give up their whole time and attention to their
toilet.   Of course it is the interest of milliners to multiply
these changes as frequently as possible, and the waste of
money thus incurred (to say nothing of higher considerations) has been a just cause of complaint with many a
husband and father.   Leaving the moral aspect of the
matter, however, out of the question, it must be confessed
that to hear a young shopman defining to his fair customers
across the counter what is 'genteel' or 'ladylike,' sounds
very ludicrous, and even impertinent.   Yet in this sort of
advice is absolutely contained the only guiding principle of
their selection.   They choose not what they like best, but
what is 'very much worn,' or what their obsequious adviser
recommends them as suitable.

Counsel of such a kind, and the easy confidence in its
worth, are, unfortunately, not confined to the haberdasher's
shop.   They seem inseparable from the purchase of every
article which, from the nature of its design or manufacture,
can claim to be of an ornamental character.   When Mater-

familias enters an upholsterer's warehouse, how can she possibly decide on the pattern of her new carpet, when bale after bale of Brussels is unrolled by the indefatigable youth who is equal in his praises of every piece in turn? Shall it be the ' House of Lords' diaper, of a yellow spot upon a blue ground, or the ' imitation Turkey,' with its multifarious colours; or the beautiful new *moiré* design, or yonder exquisite notion of green fern leaves tied up with knots of white satin ribbon?* The shopman remarks of one piece of goods, that it is 'elegant,' of another, that it is ' striking;' of a third, that it is ' unique;' and so forth. The good lady looks from one carpet to another until her eyes are fairly dazzled by their hues. She is utterly unable to explain why she should, or why she should not like any of them. Perhaps a friend is appealed to who, being a strong-minded person (with the additional incentive of a wish to bring the matter to an issue as speedily as possible), at once selects the very pattern which Materfamilias pronounced to be ' a fright' only two minutes ago. In this dilemma the gentleman with the yard-wand again comes to the rescue, imparts his firm conviction as to which is most ' fashionable,' and this at once carries the day. The carpet is made up, sent home, and takes its chance of domestic

---

* This preposterous pattern has not only been employed for carpets, but is evidently very popular, and may be noted as an instance of the degradation to which the arts of design can descend.

admiration together with all other household appointments. It may kill by its colour every piece of *tapisserie* in the room. It may convey the notion of a bed of roses, or a dangerous labyrinth of Rococo ornament—but if it is 'fashionable,' that is all-sufficient. While new, it is admired; when old, everybody will agree that it was always 'hideous.'

Glass, china, table-linen, window-curtains, tables, chairs, and cabinet-work, are all chosen on this plan. The latest invention, although it may violate every principle of good design, is sure to be a favourite with the majority. An article which dates from a few years back is rejected as old-fashioned. This absurd love of change—simply for the sake of change, is carried to such an extent that if one desires to replace a jug or a tablecloth with another of the same pattern, even a few months after the first has been bought, however good the style may have been, it is extremely difficult, sometimes impossible, to do so. The answer is always the same. 'Last year's goods, sir. We couldn't match them now.'

This state of things is the fault, not of the manufacturer, but of the purchaser. So long as a thirst for mere novelty exists independently of all artistic considerations, the aim at Manchester and Sheffield will be to produce objects which, by their singular form or striking combination of colours, shall always appear *new*. From such an endeavour some originality, indeed, results, but also a vast deal of ugliness. Now and then a good thing finds its way into the sale-room or shop-window, strikes the fancy of some buyer, and is sent home. But search for the same article next season, and you will, perhaps, find that it has been condemned to make room for some trash, which is in request, for no better reason than because nothing like it has appeared before.

For many years past there has been, as I have said, a great deficiency in public taste on such points, but by degrees people are beginning to awaken to the fact that there is a right and a wrong notion of taste in upholstery, in jewellery—perhaps in millinery, too—and in many other fields which stand apart from a connoisseurship of what is commonly called ' high art.' The revival of ecclesiastical decoration, for instance, has called ladies' attention to the subject of embroidery ; and they are relinquishing the ridiculous custom of endeavouring to reproduce, in cross-stitch worsted, the pictures of Landseer and Frank Stone. There is a growing impatience of paper-hangings which would beguile the unwary into a shadowy suspicion that the drawing-room walls are fitted up with trellis-work for training Brobdingnag convolvuli, and portraits of the once-celebrated Bengal tiger no longer appear on the domestic hearth-rug. The modern fashion of dining *à la Russe* has given a new impulse to the manufacture of dessert services and table glass; and the improved education of students in the schools of design has been attended with beneficial results in more quarters than one. Still there seems to be a great want of popular information for the guidance of those who have neither time nor inclination to study the abstruse works on various departments of decorative art which have from time to time appeared in this country.

It is hoped, therefore, that a few familiar hints on what may be called 'household taste' will not be unacceptable to the readers of this book. There is a class of young ladies who are in the habit of anticipating all differences of opinion in a picture-gallery or concert-room by saying that they 'know what they like.' Whatever advantage may be derived from this remarkable conviction in regard to music or painting, I fear it would assist no one in furnishing a house—at least, in accordance with any established principles of art. It will be my endeavour, in the following chapters, to point out those principles, so far as they have been laid down by writers of acknowledged authority, taking care to avoid all technical details in regard to manufacture which, however interesting to the specialist, would be useless to the general reader; and if I am thus enabled, even indirectly, to encourage a discrimination between good and bad design in those articles of daily use which we are accustomed to see around us, my object will be attained.

It would be hazardous to ascribe to any special cause or influence the change of popular sentiment which has since taken place with regard to architecture in this country. We may, however, not unreasonably infer that it was in a great measure brought about by the new impulse which English literature received in the early part of the present century. Indeed such an influence would not be without precedent. It was the revival of classic letters which induced the imitation of classic art. It was the love of mediæval lore, of Old English traditions, of Border chivalry, which by the magic power of association, led the more romantic of our sires and grandsires first to be interested in Gothic architecture, and then to discern its beauties. Horace Walpole, both as an author and a *virtuoso*, may be said to have sown the seeds of this taste, but it is to the writing of Walter Scott that we must refer its further development. Even in his day it was but a sentiment. The grossest ignorance still prevailed concerning the practical adaptation of a mediæval spirit to masonry and sculpture. One of the chief merits of the pointed style is that the origin of every decorative feature may be traced to a constructive purpose. Thus the stone groining over a cathedral aisle not only presents a vista of graceful curves to the eye of the spectator, but covers the area below it with an imperishable roof. The earliest promoters of the Gothic revival appreciated the superficial effect of such features without recognizing the utility which justifies their adoption. Accordingly, the glories of the ' fretted vault ' were not unfrequently imitated in lath and plaster ; nor were there men of taste wanting to praise the wretched parody.

Pugin was the first who deftly expounded the true principles of what he not inaptly named Christian art. No man of his day was better fitted to undertake the task. He was by profession an architect. He wrote with considerable ability. He entered on the subject with the full information of an earnest student and with the zeal of a religious enthusiast. There was, however, one drawback to his efforts. He blended his theological convictions with his theories on art, and the result was that the two became identified in the public mind. He had both causes deeply at heart, but he would have served both better by keeping the subjects distinct. As it was, he sometimes offended the communion he had left by needless allusions to his faith, and sometimes alarmed his fellow-Churchmen by the undue importance which he attached to the style of ecclesiastical decoration. Time has proved that the revival of Gothic architecture is due no more to the teaching of Rome than that of Geneva, and at the present day the pointed arch is almost as much in vogue among Dissenters as it is with High Churchmen. The decision of a Parliamentary Commission in 1836—that the new Houses were to be mediæval in character—gave great impetus to the growing taste; and though the Palace of Westminster may not have realized the highest qualities of the architecture which it is supposed to represent, still it has proved an excellent school for the encouragement of ancient art. It has educated many a sculptor, stone-mason, metal-worker, decorator, and cabinet-maker, who would otherwise have grown up ignorant of every phase of ornament save that which had reached him by a perverted tradition. Barry, to whose talent are due the merits of the general design, wisely entrusted to Pugin the design of those details which were to enrich his structure. Judged by the light of a maturer taste, they may appear deficient in artistic quality. But it is certain that at that time no one could have designed better.

Pugin's active and brilliant career was suddenly interrupted by a melancholy end. But long before he died, his principles had spread far and wide among the lovers of art; had been adopted and acted on by many of his professional brethren.

In the mind of the general public the spirit of mediæval design is chiefly associated with what has been called 'ecclesiastical sentiment.' But the Gothic revival is not confined to Church architecture. Indeed, if we reflect on the subject, it would seem absurd so to limit its extension. In the best ages of art there was but one style of architecture at one time for every sort of building, whether ecclesiastical or domestic. Some of the best examples of Old English Gothic which exist are certainly either churches or monastic buildings. But at the time they were raised they did not differ in style, they only differed in shape and feature, from the structures by which they were surrounded. If it be urged that dwellings of the fourteenth and fifteenth centuries are not suited to our notions of comfort in regard to arrangement of rooms, light, and ventilation, the answer is, that all these requirements are perfectly compatible with the spirit of ancient art.

There can be little doubt that the best mode of treating a hall-floor, whether in town or country, is to pave it with encaustic tiles. This branch of art-manufacture is one of the most hopeful, in regard to taste, now carried on in this country. It has not only reached great technical perfection as far as material and colour are concerned, but aided by the designs supplied by many architects of acknowledged skill, it has gradually become a means of decoration which for beauty of effect, durability, and cheapness, has scarcely a parallel. To Messrs. Minton, I believe we are indebted for the earliest revival of this ancient art in modern times. The tiles manufactured by Mr. W. Godwin have long been noted for the artistic quality of their colour and design. But for rich variety of pattern and for the skill with which the best types of ornament have been adapted for enamelled ware, plane tile pavements, mosaic and mural decoration, Messrs. Maw & Co., of Salop, stand almost unrivalled. A few specimens of their pavements and tile borders, especially fitted for household use, have been selected for illustration here, from the very numerous examples published by that firm.

When the material known as ' floor-cloth ' was first used in this country for halls and passages, its design began with an imitation of marble pavements and parquetry floors ; I have even seen a pattern which was intended to represent the spots on a leopard's skin. These conceits were thoroughly false in principle, and are now being gradually abandoned. A floor-cloth, like every other article of manufacture to which design can be applied, should seem to be what it really is, and not affect the appearance of a richer material. There are endless varieties of geometrical diaper which could be used for floor-cloth, without resorting to the foolish expedient of copying the knots and veins of wood and marble. Some very fair examples of this geometrical pattern may occasionally be met with, but, as a rule, too many colours are introduced in them. However attractive it may appear in the shop, this kind of polychromy ought studiously to be avoided on the floor of a private house. Two tints, or, better still two shades of the same tint (which should not be a *positive* colour) will be found most suitable for the purpose, and in any case there should be no attempt to indicate relief or raised ornament in the pattern.

The mural decoration of the hall is a point concerning which modern conventionalism and true principles of design are sure to clash. There can be little doubt that the most agreeable wall-lining which could be devised for such a place is marble, and next to that *real* wainscoting. In former days, when wood was cheaper than it is now, oak panels were commonly used, not only in the halls and passages, but in many rooms of even a small-sized London house. At the present time, when both marble and oak are beyond the reach of ordinary incomes, the usual practice is to cover the walls with a paper stained and varnished in imitation of marble. This is, perhaps, a more excusable sham than others to which I have alluded ; but still it *is* a sham, and ought, therefore, to be condemned. Of course, when people find themselves in a house where such an expedient has been already adopted, any alteration in this respect would involve considerable expense. But in cases where the difficulty may be anticipated, it is as well to remember that modern manufacture, or rather the revival of an ancient art, has supplied an admirable sub-stitute for marble veneering at a comparatively low price. An inlay of encaustic tiles, to a height, say of three or four feet from the ground, would form an excellent lining for a hall or ground floor passage. Above that level the wall might either be painted in the usual manner or the plaster washed with flatted colour. The latter is much more liable to be soiled than oil paint, but is much more agree-able in effect, and at a level of four feet from the floor-line would be safely removed from contact with ladies' dresses and the chance of careless finger-marks.

A cheaper and, in good hands, very effective mode of wall decoration for a hall is by distemper painting. The example here given is from a sketch by Mr. C. Heaton (of the firm of Heaton, Butler and Bayne), whose excellent taste in the design of stained glass windows and mural decoration is well known.

Mural Decoration,
executed by Messrs. Heaton, Butler, & Bayne.

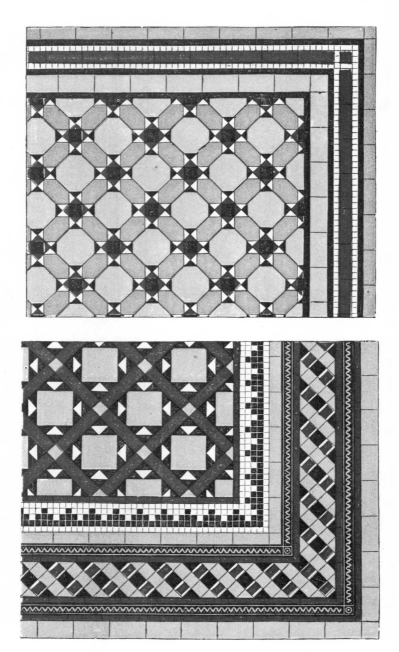

Encaustic Tile Pavements.
Manufactured by Messrs. Maw and Co.

sofa means nothing at all, and is manifestly inconvenient, for it must render it either too high in one place or too low in another to accommodate the shoulders of a sitter. The tendency of the present age of upholstery is to run into curves. Chairs are invariably curved in such a manner as to ensure the greatest amount of ugliness with the least possible comfort. The backs of sideboards are curved in the most senseless and extravagant manner; the legs of cabinets are curved, and become in consequence constructively weak; drawing-room tables are curved in every direction—perpendicularly and horizontally—and are therefore inconvenient to sit at, and always rickety. In marble wash-stands the useful shelf, which should run the whole length of the rear, is frequently omitted in order to ensure a curve. This detestable system of ornamentation is called ' shaping.' It always involves additional expense in manufacture, and therefore, by avoiding ' shaped ' articles of furniture, the public will not only gain in an artistic point of view, but save their pockets.

I am now only treating of furniture in general terms; but under this head may be discussed two important points connected with its ordinary manufacture, viz., veneering and carved work. The former has been so long in vogue, and is apparently so cheap and easy a means of obtaining a valuable result, that it is always difficult to persuade people of its inexpedience. I am aware that it has been condemned by some writers on the same grounds on which false jewellery should (of course) be condemned. But I think this is putting too strong a case. Besides, if we are to tolerate the marble lining of a brick wall and the practice of silver-plating goods of baser metal—now too universally recognised to be considered in the light of a deception—I do not see exactly how veneering is to be rejected on ' moral' grounds. The nature of walnut wood prevents it from being used, except at a great expense, in any other way than as a veneer, and when, for instance in piano cases, the leaves are so disposed as to reverse their grain symmetrically, after the manner of the marble ' wall veils' of St. Mark, the arrangement is not only very beautiful in effect, but at once proclaims the means by which that effect is attained. There are, however, many practical objections to the mode of veneering in present use. To cover inferior wood completely in this fashion, thin and fragile joints must be used, which every cabinet-maker knows are incompatible with perfect construction. The veneer itself is far too slight in substance and even when laid down with the utmost nicety, is liable to blister, especially when used for washing-stands, or in any situation where it is exposed to accidental damp. It is never worth while to buy furniture veneered with mahogany, for a little additional cost may procure the same articles in solid wood. Not long ago I had a substantial oak table made from my own design at a cost which was actually much less than that I should have paid for one veneered with rosewood or walnut. The most legitimate mode of employing veneer would be in panels not less than a quarter of an inch in thickness, and, if used for horizontal surfaces, the inferior wood should be allowed to retain a border of its own in the solid. By this means no thin edges would be exposed to injury, and the design might be treated in an honest and straightforward manner.

The subject of carved work is a more important question, because nothing but a vigorous and radical reform will help us on this point. It may be laid down as a general rule, that wherever wood-carving is introduced in the design of modern furniture (I mean, of course, that which is exposed for ordinary sale), it is egregiously and utterly bad. It is frequently employed in the most inappropriate places —it is generally spiritless in design, and always worthless in execution. The wood-carver may indeed be an artist, but the furniture-carver has long since degenerated into a machine. The fact is that a great deal of his work is literally done by machinery. There are shops where enriched wood mouldings may be bought by the yard, leaf brackets by the dozen, and ' scroll work " I doubt not, by the pound. I use the work ' scroll work ' in its common acceptation to denote that indescribable species of ornament which may be seen round drawing-room mirrors, and the gilded consoles of a pier-glass. It is not easy to say whence this extraordinary type of decoration first arose. The most charitable supposition is that, in its origin, it was intended for conventionalized foliage; in its present state it resembles a conglomeration of capital G's. Even if it were carved out of the solid wood, it would be very objectionable in design, but this trash is only lightly *glued* to the frame which it is supposed to adorn, and may indeed frequently be removed with infinite advantage to the general effect. The carving introduced in other articles of furniture is, as a rule, of a very meagre description. In fact, under existing circumstances, and until we can get good work of this kind, it would be far better to omit it altogether. It is lamentable to notice also how much the turner's art has degenerated. Even down to the middle of the last century it was employed with great advantage in the manufacture of chairs, tables, bannister-rails, &c. The judicious association of the 'bead, fillet, and hollow,' for mouldings was a simple, honest, and frequently effective mode of decoration. It still lingers in some of the minor articles of household use which have been allowed to escape the innovations of modern taste. Among these may be mentioned the common Windsor chair and the bed-room towel-horse. A careful examination of these humble specimens of home manufacture will show that they are really superior in point of design to many pretentious elegancies of our boasted nineteenth century. Indeed, I have generally found that the most common-place objects of domestic use, in England as well as on the Continent, are sure to be the most interesting in appearance. We

have at the present time no more artistic workman in his way than the country cartwright. His system of construction is always sound, and such little decoration as he is enabled to introduce never seems inappropriate.

It is to be feared that the decline of our national taste must be attributed to a cause which is popularly supposed to have encouraged a contrary effect, viz., competition. It is a general complaint with those who have the employment of art workmen, that, while a higher price is paid for their labour, its result is not nearly so satisfactory as it was prior to the Great Exhibition of 1851. That, however, is a point on which it would be beside my present purpose to enter. But it is very certain that if our ordinary furniture has cheapened in price, it has also deteriorated in quality, while the best furniture has become extravagantly dear. Some time ago I visited the establishment of an upholsterer, who announced that to meet the requirements of the public he had taken up the *specialité* of mediæval art. I inquired whether he had any drawing-room chairs in that style, and was shown some examples—rich in material, but very simple in construction. I inquired the price, and found it was no less than six guineas! Their prime cost must have been about 2*l.* 10*s.* It would be absurd to suppose that while such profits as this are demanded for every article of furniture which does not partake of the stereotyped form in use, we can ever hope for a revival of good decorative art. Any one can get drawing-room chairs designed by an architect and executed by private contract for six guineas per chair. What the public wants is a shop where such articles are kept on stock and can be purchased for 2*l.* or 3*l.* Curiously enough, in these days of commercial speculation, there is no such establishment. People of ordinary means are compelled either to adopt the cheap vulgarities of Tottenham Court-road, or to incur the ruinous expense of having furniture ' made to order.'

In attempting a solution of this difficulty, the old question of demand and supply is once more raised. The upholsterers declare themselves willing to give more attention to the subject of design as soon as the nature of public taste becomes defined. The public, on the other hand, complain that they can only choose from what they see in the shops. It is not improbable that there is a little apathy on both sides, but it is desirable that one should now take the lead, and we venture to predict that as soon as well-designed and artistic furniture is offered for sale, under proper management, there will be no difficulty in finding purchasers.

There is no portion of a modern house which indicates more respect for the early traditions of art, as applied to furniture, than the entrance hall. The dining-room may have succumbed to the influence of fashion in its upholstery; the drawing-room may be crowded with silly knick-knacks, crazy chairs and tables, and all those shapeless extravagances which pass for elegance in the nineteenth century; the bedrooms may depend for their decoration on the taste of a man-milliner; but the fittings of the hall at least assume an appearance of solidity which is characteristic of a better aim in design. No doubt this peculiarity is mainly due to the fact that, being only used as a means of communication between the street and the habitable portion of a house, it is not thought necessary that its furniture

should be of that light and easily moveable description which is deemed requisite elsewhere. It may be as well that I should call attention to two facts connected with this point; first, that although it may be desirable to make drawing-room chairs and tables conveniently light, it is no convenience to find them so light as to be fragile, rickety, and easily upset. Secondly, that there is no reasonable condition of modern convenience with which true principles of design are not compatible. The hall-table is, then, generally made of oak, in a plain and substantial manner, flanked by chairs of the same material, with a hat and umbrella-stand to correspond. Sometimes a bench is substituted for the chairs, but in any case this group of furniture is generally the best in the house, on account of its extreme simplicity.

The design given in the accompanying woodcut shows how the ordinary type of hall-table for small houses may be varied without increasing its cost, at least to any appreciable extent, and supposing both articles to be of sound workmanship and material.

I would especially caution my readers against the contemptible specimens of that would-be Gothic joinery which is manufactured in the back shops of Soho. No doubt good examples of mediæval furniture and cabinet-work are occasionally to be met with in the curiosity shops of Wardour Street; but, as a rule, the ‘Glastonbury’ chairs and ‘antique’ bookcases which are sold in that venerable thoroughfare will prove on examination to be nothing but gross libels on the style of art which they are supposed to represent. Indeed it was the practical evidence that

a fragment of genuine taste was altogether wanting. Choose
what style of furniture we may, it should surely be adopted
throughout the house we live in.

Among the dining-room appointments, the table is an
article of furniture which stands greatly in need of reform.
It is generally made of planks of polished oak or mahogany

laid upon an insecure framework of the same material, and
supported by four gouty legs, ornamented by the turner
with mouldings which look like inverted cups and saucers
piled upon an attic baluster. I call the framework insecure because I am describing what is commonly called a
' telescope' table, or one which can be pulled out to twice

its usual length, and, by the addition of extra leaves in its middle, accommodate twice the usual number of diners. Such a table cannot be soundly made in the same sense that ordinary furniture is sound. It must depend for its support on some contrivance which is not consistent with the material of which it is made. Few people would like to sit on a chair the legs of which slid in and out, and were fastened at the required height with a pin. There would be a sense of insecurity in the notion eminently unpleasant. You might put up with such an invention in camp, or on a sketching expedition, but to have it and use it under your own roof, instead of a strong and serviceable chair, would be absurd. Yet this is very much what we do in the case of the modern dining-room table. When it is extended it looks weak and untidy at the sides; when it is reduced to its shortest length, the legs appear heavy and ill-proportioned. It is always liable to get out of order, and from the very nature of its construction must be an inartistic object. Why should such a table be made at all? A dining-room is a room to dine in. Whether there are few or many people seated for that purpose, the table might well be kept of an uniform length, and if space is an object, it is always possible to use in its stead two small tables, each on four legs. These might be placed end to end when dinner-parties are given, and one of them would suffice for family use. A table of this kind might be solidly and stoutly framed, so as to last for ages, and become, as all furniture ought to become, an heir-loom in the family. When a man builds himself a house on freehold land, he does not intend that it shall only last his lifetime; he bequeaths it in sound condition to posterity. We ought to be ashamed of furniture which is continually being replaced. At all events, we cannot possibly take any interest in such furniture. In former days, when the principles of good joinery were really understood, the legs of such a large table as that of the dining-room would have been made of a very different form from the lumpy, pear-shaped things of modern use.

The annexed woodcut is from a sketch of a table in the possession of Mr. E. Corbould, dating probably from the Jacobean period. It is of a very simple but picturesque design, and is certainly sound in principle of construction. Observe how cleverly the mouldings are distributed in the legs to give variety of outline without weakening them. In the modern 'telescope' table, on the contrary, the mouldings are extravagant in contour, and the diameter of the legs is thereby reduced in some places to much less than the proper width necessary for strength. The whole ingenuity of the modern joiner has been concentrated on a clumsy attempt to make his table serve two purposes, i. e. for large or small dinner parties; but the old joiner has shown his skill in decorating his table-frame with a delicate bas-relief of ornament. And remember that it was from no lack of skill that this old table was not made capable of being enlarged at pleasure. The social customs of the age in which it was produced did not require such a piece of mechanism. In those days the dining table was of one uniform length whether a few or many guests were assembled at it, and I am not sure whether of the two fashions

the more ancient one does not indicate a more frequent and open hospitality. But be that as it may, if the Jacobean table had been required for occasional extension we may be certain it would have been so constructed, and that, too, on a more workmanlike principle than our foolish telescope slide. In like manner, if the ladies and gentlemen of King James' time had found (as probably those of Queen

Victoria's time would find) the wooden rail which runs
from end to end of the table inconvenient for their feet, it
would certainly have been omitted. As it was, they probably kept their feet on the other side of it or used it as a
foot-stool. But to show how both these modern require-

ments may be met without forsaking the spirit of ancient
work, I give a sketch of a modern table constructed in
accordance with old principles of design, but in such a
manner that it may be lengthened for occasional use at
each end, while the framing is arranged so that any one may

serve as good examples of a design which is not only picturesque in effect but practical and workmanlike as far as construction is concerned.

Without both these qualities all furniture is in an artistic sense, worthless. And they are precisely the qualities which have gradually come to be disregarded in modern manufacture. Examine the framing of a fashionable sofa, and you will find it has been put together in such a manner as to conceal as far as possible the principle of its strength. Ask any artist of taste whether there is a single object in a London upholsterer's shop that he would care to paint as a study of 'still life,' and he would tell you, not one. We must not infer from this that such objects are unpaintable simply because they are *new*. A few years' wear will soon fade silk or damask down to what might be a pleasant gradation of tint if the material is originally of a good and noble colour. A few years' use would soon invest our chairs and tables with that sort of interest which age alone can give, if their designs were originally artistic. But unfortunately our modern furniture does not become picturesque with time, it only grows shabby. The ladies like it best when it comes like a new toy from the shop, fresh with recent varnish and untarnished gilding. And they are right, for in this transient prettiness rests the single merit which it possesses.

Some years ago, when our chairs and tables were ' hand

polished,' the English housewife took a certain pride in their sheen, which was produced by a vast amount of manual labour on the part of footmen or housemaids.

The present system of French polishing, or literally *varnishing* furniture is destructive of all artistic effect in its appearance, because the surface of wood thus lacquered can never change its colour, or acquire that rich hue which is one of the chief charms of old cabinet work.

To return, however, to the question of design, it is obvious that whatever reform is attempted in the field of household taste should be in strict conformity with modern requirements, to ignore which would be sheer affectation.

The general arrangement of an ordinary English side-board is reasonable enough. It consists of a wide and deep shelf fitted with one or two drawers and resting at each end on a cellaret cupboard. If this piece of furniture were constructed in a plain and straightforward manner, and were additionally provided with a few narrow shelves at the rear for displaying the old china vases and rare porcelain, of which almost every house contains a few examples, what a picturesque appearance it might present at the end of a room! Instead of this, fashion once more steps in and twists the unfortunate *buffet* into all sorts of indescribable curves. It is bowed in front and 'shaped' at the back: the cupboard doors are bent inwards; the drawer fronts are bent outwards; the angles are rounded off; impossible

mouldings are glued on; the whole surface glistens with
varnish, and the result is—eminently uninteresting. To
fulfil the first and most essential principles of good design,
every article of furniture should, at the first glance, pro-
claim its real purpose; but the upholsterers seem to think
it betokens elegance when that purpose is concealed.
Having already touched on the subject of wood carving,
as applied to the decoration of such objects, I will only add
that whatever the faults of its modern treatment may be,
they are rendered doubly objectionable by the application
of varnish. The moment a carved or sculptured surface
begins to *shine*, it loses interest. But machine-made ornament, invested with an artificial lustre, is an artistic
enormity which should be universally discouraged.

I know no better examples of dining-room chairs
than some made in the early part of the seventeenth
century which still exist in excellent preservation at Knole
(near Sevenoaks), the seat of the Earl De La Warr, to
whose courtesy I am indebted for permission to make
several of the sketches which illustrate these pages. If
any of my readers wish to see furniture designed upon
thoroughly artistic principles, they should visit this interesting old mansion, where they may walk through room after
room and gallery after gallery filled with choice and
rich specimens of ancient furniture, most of which has
remained intact since the reign of James I. I had the

good fortune myself to discover a slip of paper tucked
beneath the webbing of a settee there and bearing an
inscription in old English characters which fixed the date
of some of this furniture indubitably at 1620. The sofas
and chairs of that period are constructed of a light coloured

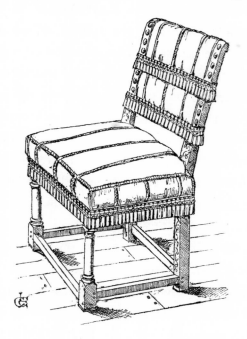

close-grained wood, the rails and legs being properly
pinned together and painted, where the framework
is visible, with a red lacquer which is ornamented with a
delicate foliated pattern in gold. The stuff with which
they are covered was originally a rose-coloured velvet,

which has now faded into a scarcely less beautiful silver grey. The backs and seats are divided into panels by a

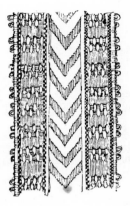

trimming composed of silk and gold thread woven into a pattern of exquisite design, and are also decorated horizon-

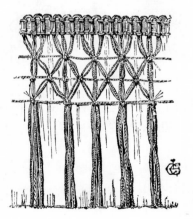

tally with a knotted fringe of the same material. The arm-chairs of the same set are of two kinds—one on-

structed with columnar legs like the smaller chair; the
other framed after a more picturesque fashion, but painted

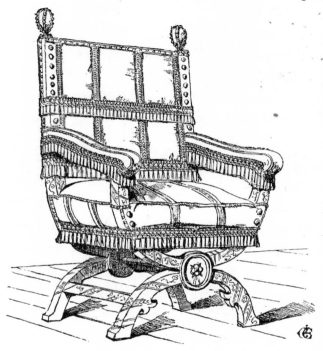

in the same style. The side rails which support the back
are studded over the velvet with large round copper gilt nails

punched with a geometrical pattern, while a larger quatrefoil
headed nail marks the intersection of the framed legs below.

A feeling is, I trust, being gradually awakened in favour of 'art furniture.' But the universal obstacle to its popularity up to the present time has been the cost which it entails on people of ordinary means. And this is a very natural obstacle. It would be Quixotic to expect any one but a wealthy enthusiast to pay twice as much as his neighbour for chairs and tables in the cause of art. The true principles of good design are universally applicable; and if they are worth anything, can be brought to bear on all sorts and conditions of manufacture. There was a time when this was so; and, indeed, it is certain that they lingered in the cottage long after they had been forgotten in palaces.

Every article of manufacture which is capable of decorative treatment should indicate, by its general design, the purpose to which it will be applied, and should never be allowed to convey a false notion of that purpose. Experience has shown that particular shapes and special modes of decoration are best suited to certain materials. Therefore the character, situation, and extent of ornament should depend on the nature of the material employed, as well as on the use of the article itself.

As for the specimens of our own peculiar national taste in textile art—the rose wreaths—the malachite marble patterns—the crimson *moire antique* with borders of shaded vine-leaves—the thousand-and-one pictorial

Dining-room Sideboard,
executed from a Design by Charles L. Eastlake.

monstrosities which you see displayed in the windows of Oxford-Street and Ludgate-Hill—they are only fit to cover the floor of Madame Tussaud's Chamber of Horrors.

It is curious that the English, who take pains that the patterns of their carpets shall be worked out with such nice accuracy, should be quite indifferent to the symmetry of their general outline. Except in the dining-room of an English house, one rarely sees such a thing as a square, or perhaps I should say a rectangular carpet. Two sides of it at least are sure to be notched and chopped about in order that they may fit into the various recesses caused by windows and the projection of the chimney-breast. This is essentially a modern fashion, and a very objectionable one. In the first place, much of the material is cut (as the phrase goes) ' to waste.' Secondly, a carpet once laid down in a room will never suit another (although it is often convenient to make such changes) without further alterations. Thirdly, the practice of entirely covering up the floor, and thus leaving no evidence of its material, is contrary to the first principles of decorative art, which require that the nature of construction, so far as is possible, should always be revealed, or at least indicated, by the ornament which it bears. No one wants a carpet in the nooks and corners of a room; and it is pleasant to feel that there, at all events, the floor can assert its independence. It is true that the colour of deal boards, especially when they become old and dirty, is by no means satisfactory, but a little of the staining fluid now in common use will meet this difficulty at a merely nominal cost.

The floors of good old French mansions were often inlaid with variously-coloured wood arranged in geometrical patterns. This branch of decorative art, known as *parquetry*, has been of late years revived in England, and is much in vogue at country houses. Parquetry floor borders are now supplied at a price which is scarcely greater per superficial foot than that paid for a good Brussels carpet. With such a border projecting two or three feet from the wall all round, the carpet need not be carried into the recesses and corners of a room, but may be left square at the sides. It is hardly necessary to say that the effect of this arrangement, including as it does the additional grace of inlaid wood-work, is infinitely more artistic and interesting than that which the ordinary system presents.

The annexed illustrations are from specimens of parquetry floors and floor-borders, manufactured by Mr. Arrowsmith of Bond-Street, whose name has long been associated with the revival of this art.

With regard to the style of the carpet, it may be assumed that, except in a few rare instances, where an European influence has been brought to bear on the manufacture of the East, all Oriental work is excellent. Care should be taken, however, to avoid those designs which are

Pavement and Tile Borders.
Manufactured by Messrs. Maw and Co.

Parquetry Floor Borders,

Manufactured by A. J. Arrowsmith.

remarkable for over-brilliance of colour. They are apt to be inharmonious with the rest of the furniture, and rich Oriental dyes frequently have a deleterious effect on the material which they stain. The crimson used in Scinde rugs, for instance, is especially destructive, and the portions dyed with this colour wear out long before the rest. The dull Indian red is far·more enduring, and is also more likely to blend well with the surrounding tints.

Turkey carpets are hardly dearer than the best productions of Brussels and Axminster, but there are some

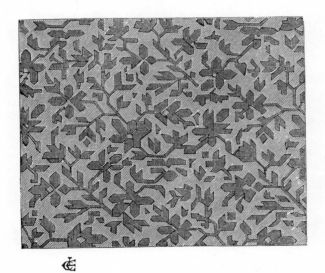

English carpets—such as those of Kidderminster—of excellent design, and of course much cheaper than any which can be imported from abroad. There is no reason

why true principles of design should not be found in the humblest object of household use, and, so far as European goods are concerned, it not unfrequently happens that the commonest material is invested with the best form and colour.   Carpets are no exception to this rule.   In London

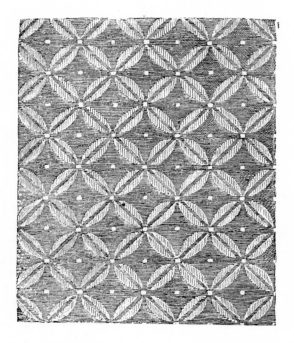

shops their artistic worth is at present a matter of mere chance, and is certainly independent of all pecuniary considerations.   The simplest diapered grounds are the best, and it is desirable that the prevailing tint of a carpet should contrast rather than repeat that of the wall paper.

In art-manufacture, it is for the shops to lead the way towards reform. The British public are, as a body, utterly incapable of distinguishing good from bad design, and have not time to enquire into principles. As long as gaudy and extravagant trash is displayed in the windows of our West-end thoroughfares, so long will it attract ninety-nine people out of every hundred to buy. But let customers once become accustomed to the sight of good forms and judicious combinations of colour, and we may one day aspire to the formation of a national taste. To attain this end, however, the manufacturers (if any are to be found so disinterested) must first inform themselves of the best sources from which good designs may be originally obtained; because at present they seem to be derived from the very worst.

But to return to my subject; the choice of a wall-paper should be guided in every respect by the destination of the room in which it will be used. The most important question will always be whether it is to form a decoration in itself, or whether it is to become a mere background for pictures. In the latter case, the paper can hardly be too subdued in tone. Very light drab, green (not emerald), and silver grey will be found suitable for this purpose, and two shades of the *same colour* are all sufficient for one paper. In drawing-rooms, embossed white or cream-colour, with a very small diaper or spot of gold, will not be amiss, where water-colour drawings are hung. As a rule, the simplest patterns are the best for every situation; but where the eye has to rest upon the surface of the wall alone, a greater play of line in the patterns may become advisable. It is obvious that delicate tints admit of more linear complexity than those which are rich or dark. Intricate forms should be accompanied by quiet colour, and variety of hue should be chastened by the plainest possible outlines. In colour, wall-papers should oppose instead of repeating that of the furniture and hangings by which they are surrounded. Some people conceive that the most important condition of good taste has been fulfilled if every bit of damask in one room is cut from the same piece, and every article of furniture is made of the same wood. At this rate the art of house-fitting would be reduced to a very simple process. The real secret of success in decorative colour is, however, quite as much dependent on contrast as on similarity of tint; nor can real artistic effect be expected without the employment of both.

Nothing is more difficult than to estimate the value and intensity of colour when spread over a large surface from the simple inspection of a pattern-book. The purchaser will frequently find that a paper which he has ordered will look either darker or lighter when hung than it appeared in the piece. For this reason it is advisable to suspend several lengths of the paper side by side *in the room* for which it is intended.

Scale: half full size.

Design for a Wall Paper.

Adapted by C. L. Eastlake from a pattern by Sano di Pietro, 1460.

The result, no doubt, will be found mathematically correct by any one who takes the trouble to measure it, but the vigour and independence of the original are utterly lost in the copy.

THE LIBRARY.

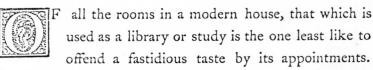F all the rooms in a modern house, that which is used as a library or study is the one least like to offend a fastidious taste by its appointments. Here at least the furniture—usually of oak—is strong and solid. The silly knick-nacks which too frequently crowd a drawing-room table, chiffonnier, or mantel-piece, are banished from this retreat. The ormolu and compo-gilt decoration which prevails up-stairs is voted, even by upholsterers, out of place on the ground-floor; and those stern arbiters of taste even go so far as to recommend a Turkey carpet or a sober-pattern 'Brussels' instead of the tangled maze of flowers and ribbons which we have to tread on elsewhere. Yet, with all these advantages, our library, especially in a moderate-sized London house, is dull and uninteresting. The book-shelves, cupboards, writing-table, and other articles of furniture which it contains, are of a uniform and stereotyped appearance, and never rise beyond the level of intense respectability. This is due to various causes, but among others to the foolish practice of varnishing new oak before it has acquired the

rich and varied tint which time and use alone can give it. Wood treated in this way keeps clean, it is true, but never exhibits that full beauty of grain which adds so much to its picturesqueness. The best plan is to rub the natural surface of the wood well over with a little oil, and so leave it. This will reveal its vein without varnish, and allow it in due course to become deeper in colour. The construction of the book-shelves themselves would appear to be simple and straightforward, and yet it is astonishing how many practical mistakes are blindly perpetuated by cabinet-makers of the present day, who have widely departed from the principles of old joinery. Of course it would be inexpedient in a familiar work like the present to point out such mistakes as are of a purely technical nature. But there are some so opposed to common sense that I cannot refrain from alluding to them. For instance, mouldings were originally employed to decorate surfaces of wood or stone, which sloped either vertically or horizontally from one plane to another. Thus, the mouldings of a door represent the bevelled or chamfered edge of the stout framework which holds the slighter panels. It is obvious, therefore, that these mouldings ought to be worked in the solid wood, and form part of the framework referred to. Instead of this, in modern cabinet work they are *detached slips* of wood, glued into their places after the door has been actually put together.

Library Book Case,
executed from a Design by Charles L. Eastlake.

To such a hold they may be sustained by little brass brackets or 'shelf-rings,' so arranged as to leave no projection which can interfere with books at the corner. The last is a modern invention, more remarkable for its ingenuity than for much practical advantage. When grooves are sunk, care should be taken to increase the thickness of the side-pieces, which otherwise become dangerously weak. The shelves themselves should never be less than an inch in thickness for a span of four feet. A little leather valance should always be nailed against their outer edges. This not only protects the books from dust, but when the leather is scalloped and stamped in gilt patterns, it adds considerably to the general effect. For material, oak is by far the best wood to use both for appearance and durability. Unpolished mahogany acquires a good colour with age. It also looks very well stained black and covered with a thin varnish. The hinges, escutcheons, &c. should then be of white metal. Stained deal, as a cheap substitute for oak, may answer in places where it is not liable to be rubbed or handled: but for library wear it cannot be recommended, since it shows every scratch on its surface, and soon becomes shabby with use. When deal is employed for economy's sake, it is better to paint it in flatted colour, because this can be renewed from time to time, whereas wood once stained and varnished must remain as it is. Indian red and slate grey are perhaps the best general tints for wood when used for ordinary domestic fittings, but these may be effectively relieved by patterns and borders of white or yellow. Sometimes a mere line introduced here and there to define the construction, with an angle ornament (which may be *stencilled*) at the corners, will be sufficient. In all chromatic decoration, I need scarcely say that bright and violent hues *en masse* should be avoided. With regard to the association of tints, it would not be difficult to quote from Chevreul, and others who have given scientific reasons for their various theories— who teach that blue is best suited for concave surfaces, and yellow for those which are convex—that the primary colours should be used on the upper portions of objects, and the secondary and tertiary on the lower. But, unfortunately, most of these precepts, however ingeniously they may be based on science, are continually belied by Nature, who is, after all, the best and truest authority on this subject. It has indeed been argued that all who consult her works with love and attention, will in time appreciate the right value of decorative colour, and that those who have learnt in that school need learn in no other. But this seems a conclusion which is not based on practical experience. The conditions of beauty in pictorial art are widely remote from those which are fulfilled in judicious decoration. An accurate knowledge of the proportions of the human form is doubtless indispensable to the loftiest inventions of the architect; but it will not of itself enable him to determine the best proportions for a building. No one is better acquainted with the subtle charms of nature's colour than a good landscape painter; but what landscape painter—as such—could be trusted to design a paper for his drawing-room wall? The blue sky which is over our heads and the green grass which springs beneath our feet would not, even if we could match the delicacy of their hues, afford us a strict and perfect precedent for the colour of our floors and ceilings; nor are the fairest flowers which bloom suitable objects to be copied literally for surface ornament. The art of the decorator is to *typify*, not to represent, the works of Nature, and it is just the difference between this artistic abstraction and pseudo-realisms which separates good and noble design from that which is commonplace and bad.

There is usually a kind of frieze running round the top of a bookcase, between the books and the cornice above them. This space may well be decorated with painted ornament in the form of arabesques, armorial bearings, and appropriate texts. Any of these would be far more pleasant to look at than the cold and formally-moulded panels into which this part is usually divided. The pilasters, also (I use the generally accepted term), which separate one compartment of the bookcase from another, might be effectively treated in the same manner.

Mantel-piece Shelves,

executed from a Design by Charles L. Eastlake.

eighteen inches in height, and divided into panels; Over this may be raised a capital set of narrow shelves—say six inches wide and twelve inches apart—for specimens of old china, &c. The plates should be placed upright on their edges, and may be easily prevented from slipping off by a shallow groove sunk in the thickness of each shelf. A little museum may thus be formed, and remain a source of lasting pleasure to its possessors, seeing that 'a thing of beauty is a joy for ever.'

The most formidable obstacle which lies in the way of any attempt to reform the arts of design in this country, is perhaps the indifference with which people of even reputed taste are accustomed to regard the products of common industry. There is many a connoisseur of pictures and of sculpture, many a *virtuoso* now haunting auctions and curiosity shops with a view to gratify his particular hobby, who would stare if he were asked to pass his opinion on the merits of a door-knocker or set of fire-irons. By such people—and they represent a very numerous class—art can only be valued as an end in itself, and not as the means to an end. The sense of pleasure, which in civilised life we derive from fair forms and colour, is to a great extent instinctive; but in so far as it is the result of education, it seems absurd to limit its range of enjoyment to this or that field of human labour. What should we think of a English amateur who is not fully competent to appreciate

Drawing-room Cheffonier,
executed from a Design by A. W. Blomfield.

pre-eminently *practical* work? Our own mechanics' work becomes mean chiefly when its ultimate object is lost sight of in an endeavour to get things up cheaply, or give them an appearance which belies their purpose.

This is especially the case with modern ironmongery and common metal work. Let us take the familiar instance of an ordinary house door, and note how the hinges are kept carefully out of sight, as if they were something to be ashamed of. It is almost impossible to construct such hinges as these which shall be of sufficient strength to support a door of any important weight. Hence the not unfrequent expense and discomfort occasioned by doors drooping at the end furthest from the hinge. The carpenter is called in, perhaps to shift the lock ' catch,' or to shave the lower edge of the door. This, of course, must leave a corresponding gap above. In course of time the hinge is partially torn from its screw holes, and a further outlay required. Now the old hinges were not ' half butts,' as our ordinary modern ones are called, but stout straps of iron, which, more or less decorated, stretched across the surface of the door on either side, and being bolted through the thickness, gave it ample support. Very beautiful examples of this hinge may still be seen on old church doors, and even in modern farm-buildings the type is still preserved, though in a ruder way. The ancient locks, too, instead of being concealed and let into the door by cutting

away, and thus weakening the lock rail, as in the modern
fashion, were boldly attached to its outer surface, and were
often, as well as the keys which belonged to them, objects

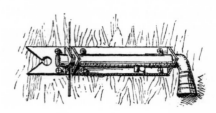

of real art in their way.   The bolts and 'spindle' handles
of the modern door are always getting out of order, besides
being thoroughly unpicturesque.   The common Norfolk
thumb-latch, used in most English cottages, is really both
a more artistic and a more practical contrivance.   Bolts
should not be let into the thickness of a door, but appear
in their proper place on its surface.

There is, perhaps, no branch of English trade more

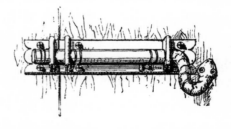

prolific in design than that of the furnishing ironmonger.
The variety of patterns which Birmingham and other
manufacturing districts supply in the way of stoves;

are elaborately vulgar. It looks like a bad imitation of rococo carved work. Almost all cast-iron ornament (excepting the delicate patterns in very low relief, such as one sometimes sees on an old Sussex stove) is hopelessly ugly. The crisp leafy decoration, and vigorous scrolls of ancient iron-work, were produced by the hammer and pliers. Bolts, straps, nails, and rivets, the proper and legitimate means of connecting the several parts, were never concealed.

Among familiar objects of household use, I do not know a more contemptible instance of perverted taste than the ordinary tea or coffee-urn of an English breakfast table. It is generally a debased copy from some antique vase, the original being executed in marble or earthenware, and, therefore, quite unfit for reproduction in metal. In order to add to its attractions, the lid and handles are probably decorated *à la Pompadour,* and to complete the absurdity, a thoroughly modern tap is inserted in the bowl. What is, after all, the use of a breakfast urn ? If it is to contain hot water, a good swing-kettle with a spirit lamp underneath is far more useful ; if it is intended to hold tea or coffee, surely a teapot or coffee-pot is a better and simpler vessel for the purpose. The same sort of pseudo-classicism may be noticed in the design of gaseliers and moderator lamps. The urn type not unfrequently reappears in them, combined with extraordinary versions of the inevitable acanthus leaf, as if in the whole range of vegetable life this was the only kind of foliage worth imitating. There is a lumpy *un-metallic* look about the ornament, which no amount of elaboration can relieve. The reason of this is that it has been either cast in separate pieces and then chased up, or (in the case of brass) stamped out of the

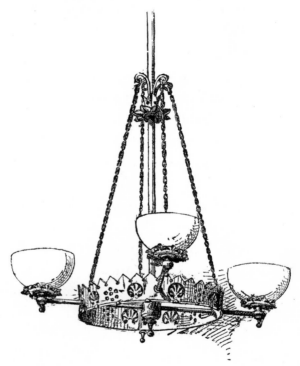

thinnest possible metal (often not thicker than a piece of paper) and then brazed together in such a manner as to look like a solid mass. Now, there can be no objection to a moderate thinness of substance in the execution of metallic ornaments. Indeed, it is, as I have said, one of the legitimate conditions to be observed in the artistic treatment of this material ; but then one ought to be able to perceive at once that it *is* thin, and quite independent of the main construction. To invest metal-work with

forms which might be as well executed in wood or stone, is to lose sight of the first principle of good design.

Both gaseliers and moderator lamps are of comparatively recent origin, and belong to those requirements of modern life with which our forefathers managed to dispense. There is, however, no reason why their design should not be treated quite consistently with mediæval principles as the annexed examples, manufactured by Messrs. Benham and Froude (of Chandos Street), will show. Specimens of work executed by the same firm are represented on the last pages of this chapter, viz. three candlesticks and two chimney-piece spill vases, made of brass, two of them being decorated with a pattern in encaustic colour. The door-bolts at page 124 are also of their design.

Public taste is often very perverse and inconsistent as to the choice and appliance of material and ornament. For instance, there was, not many years ago, a great demand for bronze candlesticks, whereas brass is a far more brilliant material for the purpose, and is capable of being treated with greater richness of form and surface-decoration. But on fire-stoves and grates, where one would think lustre and delicacy out of place, the manufacturers continue to lavish gilding and polished steel to such an extent, that one is almost surprised at the housemaid's daring to light a fire upstairs at all. Of course, the fire-irons are made to match, and it is a positive fact that in some houses each drawing-room fire-place has two pokers—a humble one for actual use, and the other, of burnished steel, kept simply to look at. It is needless to say that while such absurd practices as these continue, we can hardly hope for a healthy and vigorous development of what may be called household art.

It is, in fact, with the products of modern manufacture that we have now chiefly to deal ; and here I cannot help regretting that, owing to the apathy of the public, an excellent step towards reform in this department of art, has fallen so short of what was expected from it some few years ago.

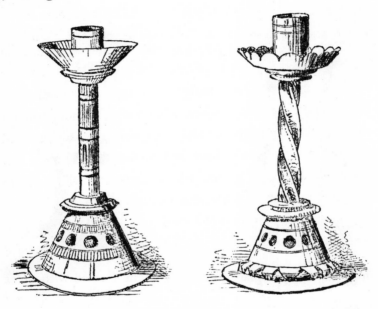

Messrs. Hardman and Messrs. Hart were, I believe, among the first who endeavoured to revive the principles of good design in connection with metal work and ironmongery, an example which has since been followed by other manu-facturers, who, like Messrs. Benham and Froude, have identified themselves with the *specialité* of mediæval metal work. The goods thus produced are infinitely superior to what is sold in the ordinary way of trade. From the most elaborate church-furniture down to the simplest article of domestic use, the work is solid and well executed. Instead of the vulgar cast-iron fenders and stove fittings which are usually supplied for the domestic hearth, we have metal which has been wrought or punched into its legitimate form. The brass candlesticks and corona lamps, the 'closing-

 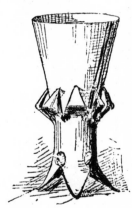

rings' and finger plates, many of them treated with great elegance of design, are stoutly made and duly polished by machinery, whereas the meretricious sheen which we see on ordinary ware is the result of nothing but a coloured lacquer, which conceals the natural hue of the brass beneath it.

It may be wondered why, with establishments of this kind in London, the British public go on buying such

trash. They also are obliged to buy whatever articles may
be 'in fashion' at the shops. Now there are degrees of
excellence in all things, and as it is just possible some of
these articles may be less objectionable than the rest, I
venture to offer a few hints which may guide the inexperi-
enced purchaser in choosing.

In the first place, never attach the least importance to
any recommendation which the shopman may make on the
score of taste. If he says that one form of chair is *stronger*
than another form, or that the covering of one sofa will
wear better than that which is used for another, you may
believe him, because on that point he can judge, and it is
to his interest that you should be correctly informed so far.
But on the subject of taste his opinion is not likely to be
worth more, but rather less, than that of his customers, for
the plain reason that the nature of his occupation can have
left him little time to form a taste at all. He neither made
the furniture in his shop nor superintended its design. His
business is simply to sell it, and it will generally be found
that his notions of beauty are kept subservient to this
object. In other words, he will praise each article in turn,
exactly as he considers your attention is attracted to it with
a view to purchase. If he has any guiding principles of
selection, they are chiefly based on two considerations, viz.,
the relative price of his goods, and the social position or
wealth of those customers in whose eyes they find favour.

Ancient Sofa,
in the Long Gallery, Knole.

The public are frequently misled by terms of approbation now commonly used by shopmen in a sense widely remote from their original significance. Thus, the word ' handsome' has come to mean something which is generally showy, often ponderous, and almost always encumbered with ornament; the word ' elegant' is applied to any object which is curved in form (no matter in what direction or with what effect). If it succeeds in conveying to the spectator a false idea of its purpose, and possesses the additional advantage of being so fragile that we cannot handle it freely without danger, it is not only ' elegant' but ' graceful.' If an article is of simple and good design, answering its purpose without ostentatious display of ornament, and pretending to be neither more nor less than it is, they only call it ' neat' in the shops. I will not go so far as to recommend every ' neat' article of household use which may be displayed for sale, but I strongly advise my readers to refrain from buying any article of art-manufacture which is ' handsome,' ' elegant,' or ' graceful,' in commercial slang: it is sure to be bad art.

The best and most picturesque furniture of all ages has been simple in general form. It may have been enriched by complex details of carved work or inlay, but its main outline was always chaste and sober in design, never running into extravagant contour or unnecessary curves. Any one who will take the trouble to examine the few specimens of

Egyptian furniture which are to be seen in the British Museum, the illustrations of ancient Greek and Roman art which have been published, or the mediæval examples which still exist in many an old sacristy abroad, and in most of our English country mansions, cannot fail to be struck with two qualities which distinguish this early handiwork from our own, viz. solidity and (what we should call) rudeness of construction.

The sofa at Knole, which dates from the same period as the chair which I have already described, is an example of thoroughly good design in its class. In the first place, its general shape is rectangular, clearly indicating the construction of its wooden framework, the joints of which are properly 'tenoned' and pinned together in such a manner as to ensure its constant stability. The back is formed like that of the chair, with a horizontal rail only at its upper edge, but receives additional strength from the second rail, which is introduced at the back of the seat. By means of an iron rack attached to each end, the sides can be raised or lowered to any angle, thus enabling the sofa to be used as a couch or a settee, at pleasure. These moveable sides, like the back, are stuffed with feathers, while the seat itself is provided with two ample cushions of the same material. A more luxurious piece of furniture—to say nothing of the richness and elegance of its external covering—could hardly have been devised, and yet there is not a single curve in its outline. After 250 years of use, this sofa is still *comfortable*, and with the exception that the velvet and trimmings are necessarily faded by age, remains in excellent preservation. It was introduced by Mr. Marcus Stone in his recently painted and very clever picture of the 'Stolen Keys,' which some of my readers may remember at the Royal Academy exhibition. Can we suppose that in the year of Grace 2118 any English artist of taste will be found willing to paint the 'elegant' *fauteuils* with which English ladies now furnish their drawing rooms? And if such a painter is forthcoming, where will he find such an object to depict? Possibly in some 'chamber of horrors' which may be devised at the South Kensington Museum to illustrate the progress of bad taste in this century, but certainly not in any private house. It is hardly too much to say that fifty years hence all the contents of our modern upholsterers' shops will have fallen into useless lumber, only fit to be burnt for firewood.

There is a notion very prevalent among people who have given themselves but little trouble to think at all on the matter, that to ensure grace in furniture, it must be made in a flimsy and fragile manner. Thus we constantly hear the expression '*light* and elegant' applied to a set of drawing-room chairs which look as if they must sink beneath the weight of the first middle-aged gentleman who used them. Now lightness and elegance are agreeable qualities in their way, and, under certain conditions of design, art should be aimed at. For instance, the treatment of mere surface ornament, such as painted arabesques, &c., or of details purely decorative and useless, as the filagree gold of a lady's earring, may well be of this character; but objects intended for real and daily service, such as a table which has to bear the weight of heavy books or dishes,

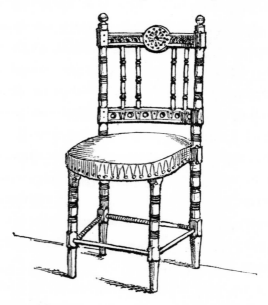

or a sofa on which we may recline at full length, ought not to look light and elegant, but strong and comely; for comeliness, whether in nature or art, is by no means incompatible with strength. The Roman gladiator had a beauty of his own, but it was not the beauty of Antinous. Our modern furniture is essentially effeminate in form. How often do we see in fashionable drawing-rooms a type of couch which seems to be composed of nothing but cushions? It is really supported by a framework of wood or iron, but this internal structure is carefully concealed by the stuffing and material with which the whole is covered. I do not wish to be ungallant in my remarks, but I fear there is a large class of young ladies who look upon this sort of furniture as 'elegant.' Now, if elegance means nothing more than a milliner's idea of the beautiful, which changes every season—so that a bonnet which is pronounced 'lovely' in 1868, becomes 'a fright' in 1869—then no doubt this sofa, as well as a score of other articles of modern manufacture which I could mention, is elegant indeed. But if elegance has anything in common with real beauty—beauty which can be estimated by a fixed and lasting standard— then I venture to submit that this eccentric combination of bad carpentry and bloated pillows is very inelegant, and, in fact, a piece of ugliness which we ought not to tolerate in our houses.

Most of us, who know anything of country life, have seen the common wooden settle which forms so comfortable and snug-looking a seat by rustic hearths. No artist who ever studied the interior of a cottage would hesitate to introduce so picturesque an object in his sketch. But imagine such a sofa as I have described in a view of the most magnificent and chastely-decorated chamber in Europe, and it would at once appear commonplace and uninteresting. Perhaps my readers may feel inclined to urge that a great deal of the interest with which we are accustomed to regard old rustic furniture is due to its age and dilapidation. It may be so; but can we expect or believe that a modern chair or couch, as they are at present manufactured, will ever, by increasing years, attain the dignified appearance of Jacobean or Tudor furniture? The truth is that our household gods become dingy under our very eyes, and the very best of them will not survive the present generation.

Now I am far from saying that we should fit up our drawing-rooms with cottage settles, or adopt any sort of furniture which is not perfectly consistent with ordinary notions of comfort and convenience. If our social habits differ from those of our forefathers, the fittings of our rooms must follow suit. But, in point of fact, there is a great deal of ignorant prejudice on these points. I know, for instance, that the old low-seated chair, with its high padded back (commonly called Elizabethan), is considered awkward and uncomfortable, simply because its proportions are strange to us. I know, too, that the 'occasional' chair of modern drawing-rooms, with a moulded bar, and perhaps a knot of carving, which chafes our shoulder-blades as we lean back upon it, is looked on as an article of refined luxury; however just because he has been accustomed to see such things all his life, they will seem right and proper in his eyes. Yet it is not a whit worse to give wood the appearance of textile fabric than to let chintz be stained and shaded like solid wood; nor is our suppositious tablecloth at all inferior in design to the pictorial absurdities which, not many years ago, we embodied in our crockery.

There is a general impression prevailing among people who are interested in the subject of art-manufacture, that well-designed furniture must necessarily be expensive. The upholsterers themselves are inclined to foster this notion, and whenever they bring out a new type of chair or cabinet which has any pretence to originality or excellence of form, they are sure to charge exorbitantly for it, because it is a novelty. Now it may, indeed, happen that what are called 'fancy' articles, being made with a view to attract the notice of individual customers, cost more than those intended for general sale, because the former are manufactured in small quantities at a time, whereas the latter are produced in wholesale lots. But it is hard that the public should have to pay for a commercial mistake due to the apathy of tradesmen. Good artistic furniture ought really to be quite as cheap as that which is ugly. Every wretched knot of carving, every twist in the outline of a modern sofa, every bend and hollow executed by the turner's wheel, has been the result of *design* in some form or another. The draughtsman and mechanic must be paid, whatever the nature of their tastes may be, and no doubt as much thought, labour, and expense of material are bestowed on modern upholstery as would be necessary to ensure (under proper supervision) the highest qualities of which the cabinet-maker's art is capable.

The drawing-room chairs of which illustrations are here

given were recently made from my design at a price which certainly did not exceed what would have been charged for such articles at any ordinary shop. I can at least testify to the excellence of their manufacture. They were made of oak, covered with velvet, and trimmed with silk fringe.

The truth is that even bad ornament is costly, and as

there is a great deal of bad ornament in modern work, it is far better, while the present state of things continues, to choose the very plainest and simplest forms of domestic furniture procurable at the shops. These will, at least, be in better taste than the elaborate deformities by which they are surrounded. That they are not always cheaper may

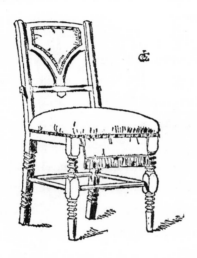

be judged from the following anecdote: A gentleman recently observed at one of the furnishing warehouses a light cane-seated chair of a very ordinary description, but the design of which, with the exception of a certain bit of ornamental carving, pleased him. He inquired the price, and was told, thirty shillings.

'And what would it cost if that ornament were omitted?' he asked. 'Thirty-five shillings,' was the answer.

Here we have a crown extra charged for the superior intelligence required from a British workman—simply to *omit* a portion of his labour. This affords some clue to the extraordinary stagnation of art-impulses in this branch of manufacture.

The natural grain of such woods as oak, rosewood, walnut, &c., is in itself an ornamental feature, if it be not obscured and clogged by artificial varnish. But where an effect of greater richness is aimed at, two legitimate modes of decoration are available for wood, viz., carving and marquetry or inlaid work. For cabinets, coffers, sideboards, and other repositories of household goods, the wood-carver's art has been successfully employed in the best ages of design; but it should be sparingly used for chairs, tables, couches, and in all situations where a knotted lump of wood is likely to prove inconvenient to the touch. It is a pity that marquetry should have fallen into such disuse, for it is a very effective and not necessarily expensive mode of ornament. It consists of inlaying the surface of one wood with small pieces of another, differing from it in vein or colour. These pieces may either be grouped in geometrical pattern, or arranged so as to represent natural objects pictorially. The *tarsiá*, or old Italian marquetry, was used for both purposes, and, owing to the minute size of the inlaid pieces, was equally adapted for either.

A certain shape is fixed upon—no one knows why—for the rail or leg of a chair, and, once executed, is multiplied indefinitely, whether by hand or by machinery, it matters little. It is made, as it were, by *rote*, and doubtless contracted for at per gross. It would be absurd to expect furniture made in this way to possess any great refinement of design.

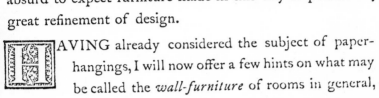AVING already considered the subject of paper-hangings, I will now offer a few hints on what may be called the *wall-furniture* of rooms in general, and of the drawing-room in particular. In most houses the chief example of this class is the mantel-piece mirror. Custom and convenience have long since determined its position, and, considering the nature of our social habits in this country, and the importance which we attach to a fire-side in almost every apartment, one can scarcely doubt that, if a glass is to be fixed anywhere on the internal walls of a modern house, this is the place for it. Unfortunately, however, while it gives apparent size and real brightness to a room, it is a feature which, as ordinarily designed, is in itself eminently uninteresting. The mere fact that it presents to the eye a reflection of every object in front of its plane is of course not sufficient to make it decorative. Accordingly we find it enclosed in a gilt frame, or, to speak more correctly, a wooden frame plastered over with composition to imitate carving of a most extravagant kind,

and then gilded—a bad style of work even if the design were tolerable. But it is usually in the worst taste. Now old frames made in the last and previous centuries, whatever their style may have been, had at least this advantage, that they were moulded and carved out of solid wood, and the difference between them and those of modern manufacture is scarcely less than the difference between well-modelled statuettes and the common plaster-casts which are sold by an itinerant image-man. We should be ashamed to place the latter on our mantel-pieces. Why are we to tolerate in one class of decorative art the vulgarities which we despise in another? If real carved work cannot be afforded, it is far better to let such mirrors be fitted in plain solid frames of wood, say three or four inches in width, enriched with delicate mouldings or incised ornament. If executed in oak, they may be left of their natural colour : if in the commoner kinds of wood, they can be ebonised (i.e. stained black), and further decorated with narrow gold stripes running transversely over the mouldings. This ought to be a less expensive, as it certainly would be a more effective, process than that of gilding the entire surface.

But we have other examples of wall-furniture to consider. The practice of hanging up oil and water-colour paintings, engravings, and photographs in our sitting rooms, is one which I need scarcely say contributes greatly to that appearance of comfort which is the especial characteristic of an English house. But it can do more than this. Independently of the intrinsic value which such works of art may possess, they become collectively an admirable means of legitimate ornamentation. Assuming, then, that the prints and pictures we wish to hang are of some artistic interest, the question arises how we can dispose them on our walls to the best advantage. Success in this respect will mainly depend on two points, viz., their judicious association, and the design of frames. The first step should be to *classify*. Oil-paintings should if possible be kept in a room by themselves. The force of their colour is always greater than that which can be attained by other 'vehicles,' and will therefore, in juxtaposition with water-colour drawings, make the latter look poor and feeble in effect. It is an old English custom to hang family portraits in the dining-room, and it seems a reasonable custom. Generally large in size, and enclosed in massive frames, they appear well suited to an apartment which experience has led us to furnish in a more solid and substantial manner than any other in the house. Besides, the dining-room is especially devoted to hospitality and family gatherings, and it is pleasant on such occasions to be surrounded by mementos of those who once, perhaps, formed members of a social circle which they have long ceased to join. But where such portraits are few in number, there can be no objection to add to this group.

Mr. Ruskin has ably brought before us the poetry of Mediæval art; Pugin and other writers have shown its practical advantages. It remains for the rising generation of architects to profit by these hints, and to show their patrons that the prevailing taste has not been called forth by the whims of a clique or the blind passion of an antiquary.

THE modern development of art is full of strange inconsistencies, and they are nowhere more apparent than in the connection of design with manufacture. Many people who are fully alive to the inartistic character of the furniture with which they surround themselves, and who would gladly hail a reform in upholstery, are deterred from helping to forward that movement by a fear that, if they did so, their chairs and tables would not be what is called 'in keeping' with the house which they inhabit. This plea, however, for tolerating the present state of things, is worthless. It would be hard, indeed, if, because the builders and land-owners compel us to live in square ugly boxes of inferior brickwork, plastered over with a delusive mask of perishable stucco, we were on that account compelled to purchase furniture as mean, as fragile, or as pretentious as our ordinary town dwellings have become. If we are to defer the consideration of household taste until we have re-modelled our national architecture, we may wait for ever.

Of late years there has, indeed, been much improvement in the design of our churches and some other public buildings, but the general aspect of London streets and suburban residences remains hopelessly uninteresting, and is likely to continue so while they lie at the mercy of speculating builders, and a system of leasehold which gives the landlord but a temporary interest in the stability of his houses.

If the style of our architecture were definitely Italian, it would naturally become a question whether we should be justified in fitting up our homes with any class of furniture but that which prevailed during the Renaissance period. But while May-fair remains what it is, a dull labyrinth of bricks and mortar, no possible standard of uniformity can help it to influence the design of the sofas and sideboards within its walls.

Yet the very people who believe in this undesirable consistency of ugliness, do not hesitate to furnish several rooms of a modern house, each after its own particular fashion, and no considerations of beauty or convenience are allowed to interfere with these conventional notions of propriety. The consequence is that our furniture generally reminds us less of its use than of trades connected with it. The great solemn dining-room, with its heavy sarcophagus-like sideboards and funereal window-curtains, is eminently suggestive of the undertaker's calling. Upstairs,

Iron Bedstead, with Canopy,
designed by Charles L. Eastlake.

all who are familiar with the conditions of good design must regard with contempt. This mistake is not confined to bed-room floors. The kitchen dresser, regarded from an artistic point of view, is really more reasonable in form and more picturesque than the dining-room sideboard; the servants' coal box than the illuminated scuttle in my lady's boudoir; and so on throughout the house. It is not, of course, the use of rich material alone, or the elaboration of ornament, but the misapplication of both, which leads to error in art-manufacture. It would be extremely absurd to use gold or silver in making a coal-box, yet these metals, even in such a situation, would be as capable of artistic treatment as iron or copper. It would be the height of extravagance to construct a side-board of cedar or sandal-wood, yet such materials could be well adapted to the purpose. But papier maché ornaments on a scuttle, or a *buffet* overladen with vicious carving and artificial sheen, have to answer a worse charge than that of mere extravagance. In the one case material, and in the other decoration, are utterly misapplied.

The design for a washing-stand which I have suggested here is of very simple construction, the only ornament introduced in it being a few easily-worked mouldings and a little inlay of coloured woods. Even if made of oak and fitted with a marble top, it ought not to cost more than an ordinary wash-stand of the same size, and would certainly be more picturesque.

A room intended for repose ought to contain nothing which can fatigue the eye by complexity. How many an unfortunate invalid has lain helpless on his bed, condemned to puzzle out the pattern of the hangings over his head, or stare at a wall which he feels instinctively obliged to map out into grass plots, gravel paths, and summer houses,

like an involuntary landscape gardener? Time was when a huge 'four-poster' was considered indispensable to every sleeping apartment, and night-capped gentlemen drew around their drowsy heads ponderous curtains, which bade fair to stifle them before the morning. Let us fancy the gloom, the unwholesomeness, the absurdity of such a custom, viewed by our modern notions of health and comfort; and remember, whatever the upholsterers may tell us, that the fashion of *our* furniture, too, includes many follies at which posterity will smile.

To the four-poster succeeded the wooden canopied bedstead, or, as it is called in the shops, the ' half-tester,' and the French bedstead, of which the head and foot-piece were in shape and size alike, and over which two curtains fell, sometimes from a pole fixed at the side, and sometimes from a small circular canopy attached to the ceiling. These forms are still in use, though iron and brass are fast displacing mahogany and rosewood, as materials in their manufacture. For obvious reasons, and especially in large towns, this is a change for the better, though I cannot help regretting that we lose the natural beauty of those woods, which frequently compensated for much bad design. The design of metal bedsteads is generally very poor, especially where anything in the shape of decoration is introduced. For instance, it is usual to conceal the joint which occurs where the tie-rods intersect each other with a small boss. A circular rosette would be obviously the most appropriate feature to introduce at this joint, whether in wrought or cast metal. But, instead of this, the iron-bedstead maker (*elegantiæ gratiâ*, as the grammarians say) insists on inventing a little lumpy bit of ornament, which, possibly intended to represent a cluster of leaves, more closely resembles a friendly association of garden slugs, and this abomination is repeated not only a dozen times in one bedstead, but in some thousands of the same pattern. The frame-work for the canopy over head is generally far too weak for its purpose, and often vibrates with the least movement, causing infinite annoyance to invalids and nervous people. In old days the outside corners of this canopy were frequently suspended from the ceiling; and this plan is still advisable when the supporting brackets are found to be ricketty. But if they were of stout iron and properly constructed, they would need no such support.

It is a great mistake to paint iron bedsteads, or any other object of metal work not exposed to the weather, in ordinary oil colour. It gives a commonplace *sticky* appearance, to avoid which *flatted* colour should be used instead.

Some of the modern brass bedsteads are of superior manufacture, stronger and better designed than those of iron. In selecting them, however, it will be well to choose those which are composed of simple bars and rods. The moment our manufacturers try to *enrich* work of this kind they lapse into vulgarities of design.

Many people now-a-days prefer, on sanitary grounds, to sleep, through the winter as well as the summer, in beds without hangings of any kind. It is difficult to conceive, however, that in a well-ventilated apartment, a canopy and

head curtains can be at all prejudicial to health, and it is
certain that they may be made to contribute not a little to
the picturesqueness of a modern bed-room. The question
of their material should of course depend on the general
aspect of the room, the nature of the carpet, wall-paper,
&c. When the colour of the latter is decided in tone,
white dimity curtains will by contrast have an excellent
effect, particularly if the dominant colour which surrounds
them is repeated in the form of braid or other trimming at
their edges. But white curtains rapidly soil in London,
and except in houses where they can be continually replaced, it will be better to let the bed-room paper be light,
and have the curtains made of *Cretonne*, chintz, or damask,
which latter materials are occasionally manufactured in patterns of very fair design. They should never be made
longer than is necessary for actual use. If they hang
within two or three inches of the floor it will be quite near
enough. When of greater length they trail upon the carpet
and get soiled at their edges, or when drawn back they
have to be looped up and pulled *over* the cord which
confines them to their place. This is a most ugly and
foolish fashion. Curtains, whether for a window or a bed,
should be simply tied back when not in use (as in Page
90   .). The disposing them in heavy and artificial folds,
such as one sees depicted sometimes at one corner of a
theatrical drop-scene or behind the ' portrait of a gentleman '

at the Royal Academy, is one out of many instances which might be quoted to illustrate the perversion of modern taste in such matters.

The canopy may be either disposed in plaits or decorated with fringe, but where plaits are used the fringe should be omitted, as it is apt to get tangled and pull the plaits out of shape. Box-plaits are the best to use, and should never be less than four or five inches in width, at intervals of about eight or ten. They should be pressed down as flat as possible, and when necessary, may be kept in shape by a stitch on either side.

Our English notions of cleanliness would scarcely permit us to tolerate any kind of coverlid for a bed which could not be periodically washed. Hence the modern counter-pane, in some form or another, is likely to remain in permanent use for our beds, though it must be confessed that both in design and material it has greatly degenerated from the quality of those made some five and twenty years ago. From an artistic point of view the counterpanes now manufactured for servants' bed-rooms, in which coloured thread is introduced for the knotted pattern on a grey or white ground, are very suggestive in colour, but I fear that any approach to this style of coverlid would be regarded as objectionable in 'best' bed-rooms.

The striped 'Austrian' blankets which have been lately offered for sale in London shops indicate a certain tendency towards the picturesque in design, but unfortunately the colours hitherto used for them are, like most modern dyes, far too crude and violent in contrast to satisfy artistic taste.

Carpets are now so universally used to cover every portion of the floors throughout an English house, that few people find themselves comfortable without one, yet there is no doubt that the old custom of laying down a bed-side rug, and leaving the rest of the floor bare, was, especially in London houses, where dust accumulates so insidiously and rapidly, a healthier and more cleanly, as well as a more picturesque fashion, than that now in vogue.

Bed-room chairs of modern manufacture are, as a rule, of simpler, and therefore of better design, than those made for the drawing-room. Some very fair examples have of late been executed for this purpose, but perhaps the best which can be found ready-made are the rush-buttoned 'nursery' chairs, of which the wood-work is stained black, with low seats and high backs. They are still to be bought in the East of London, and traditionally retain in their general shape the spirit of an earlier and better style of work than is common in more luxurious furniture.

As a lady's taste is generally allowed to reign supreme in regard to the furniture of bed-rooms, I must protest humbly but emphatically against the practice which exists of encircling toilet-tables with a sort of muslin petticoat, generally stiffened by a crinoline of pink or blue calico.

Something of the same kind may be occasionally seen twisted round the frame of the toilet-glass. They just represent a milliner's notion of the 'pretty,' and nothing more. Drapery of this kind neither is wanted nor ought to be introduced in such places. In London especially, where dust and blacks collect upon it whenever the bedroom window is open, it should be avoided. A mahogany toilet-table with marble top, and a few convenient little drawers, is a cleaner and infinitely preferable contrivance, and, though more costly at first, saves something in the weekly washing bill.

Never buy 'shaped' chests of drawers—i.e. those which bulge out in front, or veneered work of any kind, if possible. A good plan is to find out some place where mahogany furniture is made in large quantities. Order what articles you require to be made in solid wood, and either simply rubbed with boiled oil, or if they must be stained at all, let them be stained *black* before they are polished. White metal drawer-rings, &c., may then be bought of any mediæval ironmonger, and attached to the 'ebonised' wood with excellent effect.

Of course the above suggestions are only made for the benefit of those who do not care to incur the trouble and expense of ordering furniture expressly for themselves.

But an intelligent carpenter (one who does not work 'for the trade' will be best) ought by the aid of a few hints and sketches to turn out a more workman-like and picturesque object for bed-room use than the uninteresting and often weakly-constructed drawers of modern make.

For practical purposes they generally are far too deep. Every one knows the inconvenience of being obliged to delve down below innumerable strata of clothes.

It still lingers in some of the minor articles of household use which have been allowed to escape the innovations of modern taste. Among these may be mentioned the common Windsor chair and the bed-room towel-horse. A careful examination of these humble specimens of home manufacture will show that they are really superior in point of design.

FROM the earliest periods of civilisation down to the present time, there is, perhaps, no branch of manufacture which has undergone such vicissitudes of taste and excellence of workmanship as that of pottery. In ancient Greece, and within the space of a few centuries, it not only grew from a species of rude handicraft into a refined and graceful art, but declined again so emphatically in style and quality that the purest Greek vases in Pliny's time had become of immense value, and were frequently exhumed from the tombs with the same kind of zeal which inspires a modern antiquary.

In the Middle ages, Italy produced, under the general name of *majolica*, some of the most beautiful specimens of the ceramic art which the world has seen; but the excellence of that ware was continually varying, sometimes with the local materials at hand, sometimes with the chemical knowledge, and sometimes with the patronage of the day. In later times, the design of our own English pottery has been subject to like influences. The qualities which distinguish old Chelsea, Derby, and Plymouth china are well known to connoisseurs. But they are qualities which, whether good or bad, are characteristic of their age, and are not likely to be reproduced in our own time.

For many years past the manufacture of Oriental ware has been steadily deteriorating, and this fact, I fear, is in a great measure due to the increased facilities of our intercourse with India, and to the bad influence of modern European taste on native art. Ignorant people, who sneer at what they consider to be the artificial value set on quaint bits of old crockery, little know what artistic merit is frequently embodied in their designs, or by what lovely combinations of colour they excel the inventions of the nineteenth century. I believe the time will come when some of those rare examples of ancient work will be worth their weight in gold, and will be sought after, not so much to fill the cabinet of the antiquary or adorn the studio of the painter, but to serve as models for future imitation, when we shall have learnt that the principles of good design are not confined to mere objects of luxury, but are applicable to every sort and condition of manufacture. Does not Nature herself teach this great truth? The tender plants which we cultivate in a greenhouse must once have grown wild somewhere. They may surpass the flowers of our English hedgerows in fulness of leaf or delicacy of hue, but the humblest daisy or buttercup which springs on the hill-side is really a work of High Art, perfect after its kind.

NEXT to a good display of china on the table or sideboard, there is nothing which lends greater grace to the appointments of a dining-room than delicate and well-designed glass. North of the Tweed, I believe it is not unusual to regard 'crystal' as the all-important feature of domestic feasts; and certainly most London housewives who can afford the luxury are as careful of the appearance of their decanters and wineglasses as of the glittering plate which lies beside them. The same national peculiarity which makes us fastidious to secure spotless purity in our table-linen and a mirror-like smoothness for our French-polished wood, leads us also to require that every article of glass which we use shall be absolutely free from flaws or blemishes of every kind. Now it is easy to see that a demand for this sort of perfection, although it may tend to make admirable house-maids and laundresses, does not do much to promote the interests of art. I suppose there are no houses in the world kept so scrupulously clean and neat internally as a well-appointed English house ; no carriages so luxurious and well-finished in manufacture as ours ; no boots so well blacked as British boots—and yet our dwellings are un-interesting, our best equipages unpicturesque, and our dress is as ugly as that of the rest of Christendom.

Much the same might have been said up to within the last few years, and, indeed, may to a great extent still be said, of our ordinary table glass. Most householders can recollect a time when the great test of excellence in such articles depended on the question whether they were ' cut ' or not. If they were cut at all they were good ; if they were cut elaborately they were ' elegant ' ; if they were only blown they were worthless. It did so happen that at that time, bad as the cut glass was, the blown glass was rather worse ; but this may be chiefly attributed to the fact that the latter was blown into a mould, which was frequently shaped so as to imitate the effect of cutting. Our manufacturers seem quite to have forgotten that the most beautiful table glass which has ever been produced—viz., that of Venice in the fifteenth century—was not ' cut,' in the modern sense of the word, at all.

Those of my readers who have seen specimens of this exquisite and ancient art in public or private museums must be quite aware how much it differs from the heavy and inelegant vessels from which our grandfathers drank their port and sherry.

remember that such fragile objects are liable to injury and breakage whenever they change hands, and that every year must diminish their number. In addition to this fact, there was, until lately, no prospect of the manufacture being revived, and that naturally enhanced their worth. But now, when almost every characteristic of the old work can be reproduced with a fidelity which surprises even the experienced connoisseur, at about a tenth part of what it used to cost in price, it is not difficult to see that the commercial value of the original ware must to some extent depreciate.

It is not too much to say for this modest but interesting effort at reform in the manufacture of table glass, that it marks an important era in the history of industrial art. In no other direction that can be named—neither in the design of cabinet work, ceramic productions, or jewellery, have we moderns realised so nearly the tastes and excellences of a by-gone age ; and it will be a curious coincidence if, after years of humiliation and bondage, Venice should be enabled to revive one of the sources of her ancient wealth in the same epoch which has restored her to political and national freedom.

AMONG the various influences to which we may attribute the decline of artistic taste and of art manufacture during the present century, the ugliness of modern dress stands pre-eminently forward. On the painter and sculptor its effect is lamentable, compelling them, as it necessarily does, either totally to forego all representation of the age in which they live—a state of things which has never existed and could never exist in any healthy condition of art—or to undertake a difficult and thankless task, the result of which if well executed is barely interesting, and if indifferently executed is ludicrous.

The subject, although rarely considered in its æsthetic relations, has met with some degree of popular attention, and indeed may be described as one of those questions of social reform which are, from time to time, brought before the public, discussed with more or less ability, and having afforded ample scope for ingenious suggestions, are again allowed to drop into oblivion. It is the fate of our national costume—or rather let us say of European

costume (for it contains but little element of nationality)—
to be treated in this manner. Male attire in this country
is not only unbecoming, but frequently inconvenient to
the wearer, and in some respects unhealthy.

It is, however, much more easy to censure the follies of
modern dress than to propose a remedy for them, or even
to assign a cause for their existence. Take, for example,
that recently abandoned but once favourite article of ladies'
attire—crinoline. Under the names of hoop and farthingale, it was twice in vogue in this country before it was
revived for a third time in 1857. We have abundant
proof that it was both ridiculed and seriously condemned
by our ancestors. Yet neither satire nor sermons seem to
have affected its use. All that we know is the fact that
women wore it as long as it pleased them, and left it off
when it ceased to do so. But the old hoop, it will be
urged, seemed appropriate to the custom which accompanied it; it went well with patches, high-heeled shoes,
and powdered hair. Besides, it was a more honest and
less complicated affair than the modern one, and not requiring so much stuff to cover it, involved less danger to
be apprehended from fire. But is it probable that these
reasons, or any similar reasons, ensured a popularity for
the hoop or farthingale which the crinoline could not
command? Is it not a fact that, in spite of many petty
inconveniences which it occasions—in spite of its being

utterly unsuitable to the rest of a lady's toilette—in spite of the charges of indelicacy and extravagance which have been so frequently brought against it—in spite of the terrible and untimely deaths which have ensued from its use, this wretched invention continued in full favour with women for a full decade of years in the nineteenth century?

Take another instance—the modern gentleman's hat, of which the beaver prototype was introduced here about the time of the French revolution. Could anything more ugly, more incommodious, more unhealthy, more generally objectionable, be devised as a covering for the head? Yet, so far from its use being discontinued, as was thought probable during the year of the first Great Exhibition, no part of a man's dress appears to be further removed from all chance of improvement than this. No one who values his position in society—no one who cares for the public recognition of his friends—would venture to wear any substitute for it in the streets of London. Men go on enduring this evil with aching brows—just as women have endured and will again endure similar martyrdom—simply for the sake of appearances, and because, as civilised life is now constituted, singularity of dress would be considered, in most cases, a vulgar affectation.

Hopeless as reform seems to be, in certain details of modern costume, it is satisfactory to march of science.

 WELL-APPOINTED dinner-table is one of the triumphs of an English housewife's domestic care. That the cloth shall be of fine and snow-white damask; that the decanters and wine-glasses shall be delicate in form and of purest quality; that the silver shall look as bright and spotless as when it first came wrapped in tissue paper from the silversmith's; that the *epergne* shall be filled with choicest flowers—these are points which she will consider of as much importance as the dainty skill of the cook's art itself. Indeed, the general effect of a rich dinner service, or of a well-arranged buffet, contributes a more picturesque element than is apparent elsewhere, to the appointments of a modern household. But if we examine in detail the various articles which, under the general name of 'plate,' form this display, we shall find that they depend for their attraction on richness of material rather than on sound principles of design.

A sense of mere *prettiness* in decorative art belongs in some sort to our very earliest instincts. A mere baby will crow with pleasure at the sight of a gold watch or any glittering object, and try to clutch it with eager hands. In childhood the most elaborate and richly painted toys are preferred to those of a simpler kind; and, indeed, to a maturer but still natural taste the brilliant colour and complex form of manufactured objects are generally agreeable, without reference to the purpose for which such objects were designed.

The use of colour—applied by the process known as enamelling, and once so valuable an enrichment of metal work—has been long out of vogue in the manufacture of plate. The same may be said to a great extent of damascened, *niello*, and engraved ornament. A base imitation of the old *repoussé* work still lends a vulgar kind of richness to silver teapots and cream-jugs designed in the all-prevalent but objectionable taste of the time of Louis XV.; but a large proportion of modern plate is simply cast, and cast, too, in patterns which have no more artistic quality than the ornaments of a wedding cake. Take, for instance, the ordinary ' fiddle pattern' fork; can anything be more senseless than the way in which modifications of that form are decorated—now with a raised moulding at its edge, now with an outline of beads, now with what is called a ' shell,' but what is really a bad copy of the Greek honeysuckle ornament, at the end of its handle, now with a rococo scroll or a representation of *natural* flowers in low relief on its surface? All these patterns are dignified by fine names, such as the ' Albert,' the ' Brunswick,' the ' Rose,' and ' Lily.' They are reproduced over and over again at Birmingham and elsewhere. People buy them because there is nothing else of the kind to be had; but there is no more *art* in their design than there is in that of a modern bed-post. Compare them with the charming examples of antique silver which may still be seen in the windows of a curiosity shop, and observe how much we have retrograded in this department of manufacture.

Now I am not going to recommend the re-introduction of what were called ' Apostle' spoons for ordinary use. The chased figure of a saint or of a ship in full sail (a favourite termination for the fork or spoon handle of olden days) may not be the most convenient thing for the fair fingers of a lady to hold at dinner; and it must be confessed that the bowls were wider and more capacious than we require for that infinitesimal portion of soup which is served out to each guest at a modern banquet. I merely mean that the *spirit* with which this old plate was designed is extinct in our modern silver. It would be quite possible to fashion graceful spoons and forks which should also suit the most fastidious notions of convenience. A modern fork looks top-heavy because it has four prongs. Three prongs were once considered sufficient, and with three only the fork would gain in lightness and appearance. Again, the stem of the old spoon was a delicate rod, sometimes twisted and sometimes square in section. It is now flat and heavy, requiring nearly twice as much metal in its manufacture, and therefore materially increasing the cost of silver plate. It may indeed be desirable, for the sake of con-venience in handling, to keep the upper end of the stem flat, but in other respects the old shape seems preferable, and is certainly less expensive. In fact, all old plate of the best period was in-finitely lighter in weight than our own. Its chief value consisted in its design ; whereas that of the present day can but be estimated in ounces. It is perhaps for this reason that modern silversmiths prefer to load their plate with heavy *raised* ornament, instead of adopting the delicate *incised* pat-terns once in vogue.

In the whole range of art-manufacture there are few more deplorable examples of taste than the silver side-dishes, soup-tureens, cruet-stands, salvers, and candlesticks very far from what they ought to be, and the best are absurdly expensive. Perhaps the most satisfactory type is that which is commonly known in the trade as the 'Cromwell' chair. Its form is evidently copied from examples of the seventeenth century. The seat is square, or nearly so, in plan; the legs are partly square and partly turned; the back slopes slightly outwards and presents a padded frame, stretched between two upright rails, to the shoulders of the sitter. Both the seat and shoulder-pad are stuffed, or supposed to be stuffed, with horsehair, and are covered with leather, studded round the edges with brass nails. Sometimes the material called 'American cloth' is substituted for leather. Some time ago I saw a set, or as the shopkeepers delight in calling it, a 'suite,' of this kind in Tottenham Court-road, at two guineas per chair. There were also some arm-chairs corresponding in material (though not exactly in design) which were offered at 5*l*. a piece. Considering that the wood employed was oak, this was certainly cheap compared with the prices of more fashionable establishments. But not long afterwards an architect showed me a design which he had made for an arm-chair cleverly carved in oak and very comfortably padded. It was well executed in the country for five guineas. In London the order would not have been undertaken for less than ten. But in general form, at least, it might be picturesque and sturdy, and these are just the qualities overlooked by cabinet-makers and joiners in their work, which is generally frail and uninteresting.

Mother-of-pearl handled knives and forks for dessert may now be bought at a very reasonable price, and are far more agreeable to the touch, as well as in appearance, than those made entirely of silver or plated metal, which are generally of very poor design. Mother-of-pearl, moreover, does not discolour with age, like bone or ivory.

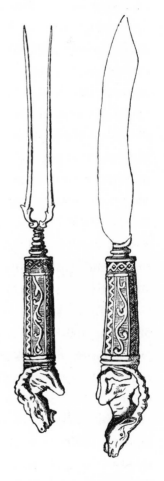

A slight improvement may be noticed in the recent design of some small articles of table service, as mustard-pots, salt-cellars, and cruet-stands, but as a rule they are far inferior, both as regards taste and execution, to those which were manufactured not only at the best time, but early in the last century. Indeed, if I might venture to offer any direct advice of the kind which one constantly sees associated with catchpenny advertisements, and addressed to 'persons about to furnish,' I should suggest their buying plate, not at the magnificent emporium of Messrs.

So-and-so—where the eye is perplexed by a hundred and fifty pretentious vulgarities fresh from Sheffield or Birmingham—but rather at some of the old jewellery-shops in Hanway Street or Wardour Street, in which articles of old silver are still sold, far better in design, and at a cost rarely exceeding that which is paid for modern plate of the same intrinsic value. Some of the mediæval metal-workers have, it is true, attempted to revive the ancient taste and dignity of the silversmith's art; but while they charge for their goods a price which is at least treble that of the ordinary trade, we can hardly expect them to be patronised by the public at large. A good simple design ought not to involve more labour in execution than a bad elaborate design, supposing both to be equally well executed; and the execution of ordinary ware is at least good enough for all practical purposes.

The future success of art-manufacture in England must, of course, depend in a great measure on the taste of the public for which it is supplied; but I do not see how that taste is to be thoroughly and popularly reformed until manufacturers begin to educate it, by the production and display of goods which will bear the test of sound criticism. Museums and exhibitions of art treasures are useful in familiarising the eye with the appearance of objects which illustrate excellence of ancient skill. But it must be remembered that such objects are usually articles of luxury, which at any period would lie beyond the reach of ordinary means, and which in many instances were applied to some purpose that has long since fallen into disuse. In examining them, we are apt to forget that our forefathers were not all people of unlimited wealth, who could afford jewelled caskets, costly embroidery, richly carved cabinet work and plate, which would fetch ten times its weight in gold and silver.

In those early days there were, as now, households in which economy was an object. Pots and pans, wooden trenchers and three-legged stools—articles, in short, far more humble in make and material than those which increased commercial prosperity has given to our present homes—were then required, produced, and sold at a moderate price. But it was not because they were cheap that they were necessarily ugly or ill-fashioned. That contemptible kind of workmanship which is at once slovenly and tasteless because it may be showy and cheap, was not then in demand. The rich, indeed, spent more money, both on dress and objects of general luxury, than at the present day ; but such furniture as befitted the habits of ordinary citizens and country gentle folks of that date was found in the homes of the middle classes more than two hundred years ago ; and wherever it existed, we may be sure it was deftly and honestly made. Those examples of ancient handicraft which have reached our own time may well put to shame the efforts of modern smiths and cabinet-makers who work like machines, while their ancestors worked like artists and practical men.

It would be absurd, however, to suppose that English brains have deteriorated in the same proportion as English taste. Our artisans have as much intelligence as ever; it only wants proper direction and employment. At present both master and man are so accustomed, from their youth up, to false principles of design and execution, that it requires some stern teaching and no little patience to lead them back to their proper groove of work. Meanwhile, the public must do their part. If they will insist on the perpetuation of pretentious shams—if they will prefer a cheap and tawdry effect to legitimate and straightforward manufacture—no reform can possibly be expected. But if they encourage that sound and healthy taste which alone is found allied with conscientious labour, whether in the workshop or the factory, then we may hope to see revived the ancient glory of those industrial arts which, while they derive a certain interest from tradition, should owe their highest perfection to civilised skill.

Drawing Room by Eastlake

An "Eastlake" Organ, by Mason and Hamlin
Philadelphia Centennial

Part II
The House Beautiful
Essays on Beds and Tables, Stoves and Candlesticks
by Clarence Cook
New York 1877

INTRODUCTION.

A MONG the smaller facts that must be taken note of in drawing the portrait of these times is the interest a great many people feel in everything that is written on the subjects of house-building and house-furnishing. There never was a time when so many books written for the purpose of bringing the subject of architecture—its history, its theory, its practice—down to the level of the popular understanding, were produced as in this time of ours. And, from the house itself, we are now set to thinking and theorizing about the dress and decoration of our rooms: how best to make them comfortable and handsome; and books are written, and magazine and newspaper articles, to the end that on a matter which concerns everybody, everybody may know what is the latest word.

When those who have attempted to instruct the public on so intimate and personal a subject have looked about for authorities and models, they have turned back with one consent to the past, and either adopted the usage of old times as a whole, or made it a basis for their suggestions, a text for their sermon. But, if we ask where the old-time people found their models, we certainly do not get for an answer, that they ran to this or that book for them, or that they sought the advice of this or that architect. Whatever they did, were it good or bad, came out of their own minds, and was suggested by their own wants, and represented their own taste and sense of fitness.

Now, we have the same faculties that the men who lived before us had, just as we have the same desires and needs, and we have only to go to work in the same way in order to produce the same results.

Just let us consult our own desires and needs, and refuse to be governed
by those of other people. And let us refuse to take what is offered
to us, if it does not suit our needs or our purses, and learn not to fear
being sent to Coventry for our refusal.

The best plan is to know first, as near as may be, how we ought
to live externally, and then to surround ourselves with the things best
suited for that mode of life, whatever it may be. This, however,
commonplace as it sounds, is so seldom done, that it must be thought
a thing extremely difficult to do. Look about you, reader, and ask
yourself, how many people you know who live as they really like to
live, and let the world go by. There are such people. I know such
in my own circle, but there are not many of them, and it certainly is
not the way of the world at large. But, whoever will try the experiment will find the reward in peace, and serenity, and real comfort, so
abounding, that it will be no longer a query with him whether he shall
continue it or not. And he will find that the question of furniture
will disappear from the catalogue of vexations, because there is always
provision in the world for every reasonable want. Every country,
too, has its own models, and was at one time satisfied with its own—
that is, the mass of the people were satisfied, though in every country,
at all times, the rich have preferred something borrowed and exotic.

> "I would give thilke Morpheus
>   *   *   *   *   *
> If he woll make me sleepe alite,
> Of downe of pure doves white
> I woll give him a feather bed,
> Raied with gold, and right well cled
> In fine black sattin *d'outremere ;*
> And many a pillow, and every bere,
> Of *cloth of raines* to slepe on soft,
> Him there not need to turne oft."

Their satins must come from over seas, and homespun will not do,
but they must go for cloth to some foreign town of Rennes, else they
cannot rest in their beds. But the charm of every house is to find
the people in it self-contained, and taking their pleasure and their
comfort where they can, in the things that come to them, rather in
what they have had to seek painfully and far.

Yet it is not worth while to ignore the fashion altogether, nor to insist on having things entirely different from those our neighbors have. I know there is a great deal of ridicule expended upon people who follow the fashion; but we ought to reflect that not to follow the fashion (the question is now of ways of living, of dress, and of manners) is found, in the long run, to be expensive, not only in money, but in time, and really takes away our attention too much from matters better worth while. The young man who gave his whole mind to the tying of his cravat could not, of course, give any of his mind to higher things; and if we fuss too much, or fuss at all, for that matter, over our coats, and trowsers, and gloves, and hats, we soon find we are on the wrong road. It is no better to worry ourselves over our house-furniture, and to insist upon having ideal and faultless surroundings. If we have things about us different from what the way of the world provides, it ought to be because we came across them naturally, and liked them, not because we were trying to be peculiar.

This is the good general rule, and the following it would help settle many difficulties that we hear people complaining of every day. Much of the trouble we have in getting furniture to suit us comes from our wanting things that do not suit us. We must have something that somebody else has or has not. We must either follow the fashion or lead the fashion. The last thing we think of is to please ourselves. A young couple heroically determined that when they were married they would live as comfortably as they could on the smallest income that would be theirs; and that for no fashion's sake, nor for any fidgety conventional friend's sake, would they go to any expense that would give them a minute's uneasiness. The husband was a professional man, fond of books and pictures; the wife was womanly, pleased in her own work, in her books and stitchery, and could touch the piano; and when evening came was pleased with what pleased him. "Flats" had not yet been introduced, and between a "whole house" and a boarding-house (the latter the last resort of despairing young married people) there seemed no middle ground, nor was any, until it occurred to one of them—they never could tell which one it was to whom the happy thought was due—to take a whole house and live in the upper floors, and, reserving a corner of the cellar for coals, to let the rest of the house to somebody else. This they did, and straightway went to work to furnish their floor with the best-looking furniture they could get without hunting too far. In the artist circle, and the circle of young lawyers and budding literary folk, and architects, and the Utopians generally, this upper floor became a synonym for domestic paradise; and, indeed, a prettier place had not then been seen in New-York. But it soon became whispered abroad —that is, in the course of two years or so—that anxious friends, moving in the upper circles of society, and sadly missing the aid and comfort these two were to have brought to those benighted regions, had so fretted and worried these happy young people, and had teased them so about the world, and what it was saying, and what it was thinking about doing, that at last they wearily succumbed, and let a fine house be bought for them, as ugly and anti-domestic as a New-York brown-stone front knows so well to be; and there they went, and there a charming and successful experiment came to a common-place ending.

Suppose this an imaginary story; but it is a type of the trouble everybody finds in living in his own way. Society does not regard with approval such departure from the common road, and the ruts are made so easy for us all to roll along in, there is small temptation to risk upsetting by trying unaccustomed paths.

However, my purpose is not to recommend eccentricity, nor even a modified Bohemianism. I have no mission to preach a crusade against luxury and bad taste; nor have I a hope that anything I can say will bring back simplicity and good taste. I am not at all sure that my own taste is good, or that I can depend upon its being good at all times. If I am pushed to the wall with a question as to my right to be heard in this matter, I can only say that, after much tribulation, I have reached a point where simplicity seems to me a good part of beauty, and utility only beauty in a mask; and I have no prouder nor more pretending aim than to suggest how this truth may be expressed in the furniture and decoration of our homes.

CHAPTER I.

THE ENTRANCE.

A FEW words, in the beginning, about the "Hall," as, in our American love of fine names, we are wont to call what, in nine cases out of ten, even in houses of pretension, is nothing but an entry or passage-way. A hall *(aula)* must be a large room, large at least in proportion to the size of the house; and such a hall it is rare to see in our modern city houses. Our old-fashioned houses had often halls; I remember some in houses about the Common in Boston, and some in old towns like Gloucester and Hingham, that were handsome, and that, seen to-day, give a pleasant idea of the comfort and substantial elegance enjoyed by many not over-rich people in old times, when the population was not so thick as it is to-day. In city houses, particularly in New-York, where I believe we are more scrimped for room, and where even the richest people are obliged to squeeze themselves into a less number of square feet than in any other city in the world calling itself great, there is often a sufficient excuse for these dismal, narrow, ill-lighted entry-ways, but there is no excuse for them in our country houses. As in meeting a man or a woman, so in entering a house, the first impression generally goes a great way in shaping our judgment.

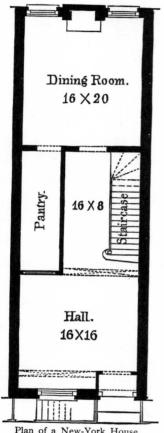

Plan of a New-York House.
No. 1.

If, on passing the door, we find ourselves in a passage six feet wide, with a hat-stand on one side reducing it to four feet, and the bottom step of the staircase coming to within six feet of the door-way in front of us, and a gaselier dropping to within a foot of our head, we get an impression of something that is not precisely generosity, and which is not removed either by finding the drawing-room overfurnished, or by the fact that the hat-rack was made by Herter, that the carpet on the stairs is Wilton, and that the gaselier is one of Tiffany's imported masterpieces.

Of course, none of us are to blame for the smallness of our entry-ways. Our landlords must be called to account for this defect, and all they can say in excuse is, that house-building is a thing partly of necessity and partly of fashion. "When there was ground enough," the landlords will say, "when lots 25 x 100 were the rule, and not, as now, the exception, we built good-sized

Faience Cistern.
No. 8.

"She 'll be down in a minute, sir."
No. 2.

houses and gave wide enough halls; now that people are obliged to be content with two-thirds of a lot (houses sixteen feet wide being common in New-York), it is not possible to have anything but narrow entry-ways—a hall is out of the question." This is not exactly as the landlords say. There are houses in New-York—I once had a friend who lived in one, and I always recall the little box with pleasure —which, though among the very smallest, are better provided in the way of hall than many of the largest dwellings. The house I speak of had an entry that might fairly be called a hall, for it was sixteen feet wide, and nearly as long: the accompanying plan (No. 1) will show how it was obtained. The house was sixteen feet wide, and, as will be seen, the first floor was taken up with the dining-room, pantry, staircase, and the hall. The second floor had two rooms, one in front and one at the rear, with a large open hall (not a dark room) between them, and above were the bedrooms in two stories.

All I am concerned with now is the arrangement of the first floor, which seems to me, if we must have small houses, one that met satisfactorily the demands both of comfort and of good looks. On entering the front door—the house was what is called an "English basement," and the sill of the front door was only eighteen inches from the sidewalk —we found ourselves in a narrow vestibule, the outer door of which was always wholly or one-half open. The inner door being passed, there was a generous, hospitable space, which was thus disposed of. The vestibule was, as the reader will see, taken off this open space, and the recess formed by the left side of the vestibule and the left wall of the house was used as a bay-window to be filled with plants. Against the right-hand wall there was nothing placed, in order that the line from the front door to the stairs might be unobstructed, but some framed engravings were hung there, while against the opposite wall, was a table with a generous mirror—for, to parody Emerson, "All mankind loves a looking-glass"—and pegs for hats, and a rack for umbrellas. A settee stood against the end wall of the pantry, and this was all the little hall contained. With its ample space, its dark painted and shellacked floor shining beyond the edges of one of those pretty rugs made in Philadelphia of the clippings of tapestry carpets, its box of ivy in the window, its shining mirror, and its two Braun autotypes, I am sure there was no hall in the city, no matter how rich the man it might belong to, that had a more cheerful, hospitable look than that of my friend's house.

Even there, however, pains were taken to keep everything down. Sixteen feet square is a sizable hall, but it may be made to look small—as any room may—by being furnished with things out of proportion. Heavy-framed pictures or engravings on the walls, or sprawling patterns on the oil-cloth or the carpet, large pieces of furniture, fashionably clumsy, gawkily designed *à-la-mode*, and a bouncing gaselier in mid-air, will make a mere cubby-hole out of a room which by judicious treatment could get full credit for all its cubic inches. Remembering this, the hall I speak of was furnished with only those things that were really needed (the plant-stand and the prints must be excepted), and these were made to suit themselves to the situation. The mirror was a large, generous-looking affair

(almost a horse-glass, as the English cabinet-makers of
the last century translated *cheval*-glass), and the shelf
under it was rather long and narrow,—a shelf of mahogany

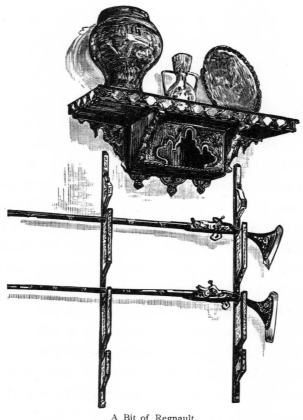

A Bit of Regnault.
No. 3.

supported on brackets of the same wood. The hat-and-
umbrella-rack was an affair of the same sort as the Moorish gun-rack shown in cut No. 3, with pegs for the hats,
and rests for the umbrellas and canes.

CHAPTER II.

THE LIVING-ROOM.

I USE the word "Living-Room" instead of "Parlor," because I am not intending to have anything to say about parlors. As these chapters are not written for rich people's reading, and as none but rich people can afford to have a room in their houses set apart for the pleasures of idleness, nothing would be gained by talking about such rooms. I should like to persuade a few young people who are just pushing their life-boat off shore to venture into deeper and more adventurous seas, that it will make their home a great deal more cheerful and home-like if they concentrate their leisure, in-door hours in one place, and do not attempt to keep up a room in which they themselves shall be strangers, and which will make a stranger of every friend who comes into it. Happily, the notion that such a room is absolutely necessary to every respectable family is no longer so prevalent, nor held so binding as it once was. A good many people who were children in New England fifty years ago will remember the disagreeable parlor of the period, into which they were only permitted to go on Sunday afternoons, though they often forgot to go there

Let us begin, then, with the frank abandonment of any formal parlor, but, taking the largest, and pleasantest, and most accessible room in the house, let us give it up to the wife and children in the day-time, and to the meeting of the whole family when evening comes.   There is not much need at the present time to emphasize this suggestion, for it is one which experience and necessity have already made to a good many people; and now that the problem " How to get a dwelling at a rent within moderate means" is being solved by the increase of "flats" and "apartment houses," the "parlor" must be given up, there being no provision made for it in the common plans.   But it is by no means my notion that the living-room should be a homely, matter-of-fact apartment, consecrated to the utilities, while the Muses and Graces are left to amuse themselves in the hall.   On the contrary, we want in the living-room, for a foundation, that the furniture shall be the best designed and best made that we can afford, all of it necessary to our comfort, and intended to be used; not an article to be allowed that does not earn its living, and cannot prove its right to be there. These wants being first provided for, we will then admit the ornament of life—casts, pictures, engravings, bronzes, books, chief nourishers in life's feast; but in the beginning these are to be few, and the greatest care is to be taken in admitting a new-comer.   The room ought to represent the culture of the family,—what is their taste, what feeling they have for art; it should represent themselves.

Just a word more as to the color of the rugs to be employed. The Eastern designers know too much, or have too correct an instinct, to use a great deal of white in their designs; they get all the light and brightness they want without it, and even when they use white it is not pure white, but gray, and used with extreme economy at that; at least in all the successful carpets. It is true, these Eastern carpets are sometimes found with what is called a white ground, and these are among the handsomest, especially when they come from Persia: but the white, in the first place, is not white, but some tint that only looks white by force of juxtaposition, and, then, what there is of it is used in so bold a way and so broken up, that all we feel, in looking at it, is, that it is cheerful and festive, whereas the Eastern rugs we are most used to seeing, and especially the Turkey rugs, are somber and rich rather than gay. However, a "white ground" carpet is rather a holiday friend, and is not to be recommended unless the room it is intended for be a darkish one, or the character of the household be such that it will not be subjected to the ravages of children and husbands with dirty boots. Otherwise, choose a thick rug with a pattern a good deal broken, and with nothing very odd or noticeable in the design, and let it take its fortunes. If it be only used and not abused, it will improve with time, and outwear more than one Brussels carpet.

If people object to rugs, there is at least the comfort left them of knowing that they can get carpets better made than ever carpets were before, and with designs that can

only be matched for elegance and beauty with those of
Persian rugs.   These are English carpets, designed and
made by the houses of Morris & Co. and Cottier & Co.
These carpets are so handsome and so well made, that, if
one can afford it, I would advise having squares made of
them, with the borders that are sold with them.

There are, however, other and cheaper resources.   They
make, in Philadelphia, a pretty and serviceable rug out of
the ravelings of fine carpets, and in Boston I have seen the
same material.   There is, of course, no set pattern, but a
pleasant mingling of hues, and the texture makes it agreeable to the foot, though it is, perhaps, more comfortable as
a rug over a matting in summer, than as a sole dependence
in winter.   Still, it is something it is well to know of.
These carpets come in breadths, like common carpeting,
and can be made into rugs of any size.   They have no
"right" side, but can be turned at pleasure, and the edges
will not curl up as those of rugs made of ordinary carpeting are apt to.   Those manufactured by William Pollock,
carpet manufacturer, 937 Market street, Philadelphia, second
door below Tenth street, are highly recommended, and they
are also made by some firm in Providence, Rhode Island.
They make, in Scotland and in Holland, a carpeting of a
mixture of wool and jute, which is dyed a deep maroon,
and is about the thickness of Brussels carpeting.   A good
way of using this is to make a square or parallelogram
the size of the clear space of the floor when all the large
pieces of furniture are in their places.   This is laid down
and held in its place by rings sewed to the under edge,

-rid of upholstery and stuffing in our furniture as far as possible. The wooden chairs, and chairs seated with rushes or cane of the old time, were as comfortable as the stuffed and elastic seats we are so fond of. And if we could

Sofa, with Movable Cushions.
No. 12.

consent to come back to something of the old-fashioned austerity, we should find it greatly to our profit in many ways. I do not believe a more comfortable chair can be found than a pattern once in universal use here, but now only seen in old country homes. The seat was of wood, hollowed, and curved as skillfully as if it had once been of soft material, and had been molded to its perfection by an owner of persistently sedentary habit. The seat sloped a little from the front to the back, as every chair-seat ought; was of ample depth, and was inclosed by a slightly sloping back and gently spreading arms. The back was composed of slender rods, and the flat arms were a little broadened and rounded at the ends, offering a pleasant and soothing

object for the hands to play with. The legs of these chairs
flared considerably, but only so much as to give the necessary stability, and they were connected by rungs. Now
these chairs, once in common use all over our eastern
country, and then despised in the growth of luxury and the
desire for stuffed furniture, are come into favor again, and
are bought up at once wherever they are offered for sale.
It is well known, too, what a prosperity the Wakefield
manufacture of rattan furniture is enjoying, and it deserves
it too. Whenever the designs obey the law of the material
employed, and do not try to twist or bend it out of its
own natural and handsome curves, they are sure to be
pleasing to look at and serviceable to use. The Chinese

The same, without Cushions.
No. 13.

make a picturesque and comfortable chair out of the large
shoots of bamboo, and their reclining chairs, with a foot-
rest that can be pushed out or in at pleasure, are almost
indispensable to a house in the country. With such a

chair, and a good hammock, a hermit might set up housekeeping. It would be hard for him to say what he wanted
next. Diogenes would have said he wanted nothing but
to throw away the hammock. And, indeed, the chair I
speak of is bed and table and chair all in one. Further
on, the reader will find a cut of one of these chairs. A
sofa, or settee, that seems to me to answer all one's
reasonable needs, is shown above, in cuts Nos. 12 and 13.
It is long enough to lie upon and take a nap, and deep
enough and low enough to sit upon with comfort. The
cushions are all movable at need, and in summer, if we
choose, we can stow them away and use the sofa as a
settee. As for the coverings of the cushions, we need not be
at a loss, for there has not been in the last fifty years such
a supply of materials for this purpose as there is to-day:
the stuffs themselves of first-rate make, and the designs as
good as ever were produced at any time. We have serges
nowadays, in colors whose delightfulness we all recognize
in the pictures that Alma Tadema, and Morris, and Burne-
Jones and Rossetti paint, colors that have been turning all
the plain girls to beauties of late, and making the beauties
more dangerous than ever—the mistletoe-green, the blue-
green, the duck's-egg, the rose-amber, the pomegranate-
flower, and so forth, and so on,—colors which we owe to
the English poet-artists who are oddly lumped together as
the Pre-Raphaelites, and who made the new rainbow to
confound the scientific decorators who were so sure of what
colors would go together, and what colors would n't. Whoever would get a new sensation, and know for the first

time what delicate or rich fancies of delightful color and softness of touch can be worked with silk and wool, must go to the Messrs. Cottier's shop and learn for himself.

A Settle, convertible into a Table.
No. 14.

It may sometimes happen that a larger table than ordinary may be much needed when maps are to be consulted, or large books examined, or a collection of prints enjoyed by a company of amateurs. Yet, the room is not large enough to permit of such a table standing in it all the time. The common ironing-table of our kitchens, the "settle" of the old days, has served Mr. G. F. Babb made his success, as it is of all success. And he had enough of the artist in him not to allow himself to be tempted into fantasticalness by the demands of fashion. For if we are to believe the report of the fashion-prints of the day, there never was greater fantasticalness than in the dress of the time, yet even when frippery and furbelows were at the height of their absurdity, the furniture kept a staid and discreet appearance, as much as to say: "We can't both of us be giddy; it rests with me to uphold the dignity of the times."

To the eye of one whose liking for our Revolutionary furniture is not a new thing, the charm of it consists, apart from its usefulness, which is evident to everybody, in the color given to it by age, and in the simplicity with which all its ornament is obtained. Its moldings are always good and quiet; just what is needed, and no more, to round an angle with elegance, and to catch the light agreeably, and whenever any carving is attempted, or paneling, there is a certain moderation in it that is very refreshing in these loud times. Yet they are not too tame either, but their spirit is the spirit of high-bred people, and not of folks who like to be conspicuous. Even the architectural details in bureaus and clothes-presses that these old people were so fond of,—a little too fond, per-haps,—were often very delicately and adroitly managed, and we find ourselves easily forgiving them, seeing how well in keeping they are with the effect of any piece as a whole. Yet, much as these articles of furniture deserve to be praised, I would not counsel that they should be copied. In fact, I do not believe in copies, whether of furniture, of pictures, or of men and women. Nothing ever can be copied exactly, and we ought never to try to do it, unless it be for purposes of instruction, and even then its desirableness may be disputed. The least thing from a master's hand is pretty sure to be better worth studying, if we would know something about the master's method of

For Books, or Work, or Healthful Play.
No. 28.

working, or his way of thinking, than the best copy. And it may be said that the better artist the copyist is, the less his copy is apt to resemble his original. The French have carried the copying of old work—in furniture, in jewelry, in pottery—to great perfection; but an artist would rather have a square foot of genuine mediæval or Renaissance carving than the best copy of a whole piece that ever the skill of Récappé produced. So with old American or English furniture (for how much was made here, or how much imported, we do not know); no matter how super-ficially resembling the copies may be, they will always be wanting in something,—in proportion, in delicacy, or in spirit. And even if copies could be cast in a mold, it is not good to wish for them, for we can put all their merits into original pieces, made for ourselves to-day, that will not only give us pleasure, but will show our children that we knew how to profit by what our fathers taught us.

Cuts Nos. 28 and 29 are suggestions of designs for tables that will be found convenient for the living-room. No. 28 is rather intended to go against the wall, to write at, or hold the books and pamphlets that are being read, while the two shelves below will be found very convenient for folios, and large books of prints, atlases, etc., etc. A shelf at one end pulls out at need. In design, the lower supports of the table are heavier than need be, and the lower shelf, also, much too heavy. Cut No. 29 is intended for the center of the room, and ought to be a handsome piece if well carried out. It was designed for me by Mr. George F. Babb, who is so much of an artist, and puts so much thinking into his work, that I believe he will make no objection to my criticising his table a bit, and objecting to the three small brackets that support the projecting top at the ends. As will be seen by the drawing, these brackets are not the ends of straps that brace the two supports of the table and help to steady the top. There are no such straps, and perhaps they are not needed, but these little brackets are certainly not needed, and being useless and yet looking as if they were useful, they ought

to have been omitted.   But this is a small matter, and
would not be worth mentioning, if it were not for the
tendency there is nowadays to add to furniture just such
little points as these, that are intended for decoration, yet
do not decorate, and that look as if they were a part of
the construction, yet, in reality, have nothing to do with
the construction.   This point settled, the reader will no
doubt enjoy with me the skill with which Mr. Babb has

A Criss-cross Table.
No. 29.

contrived to get a variety of lines pleasingly united in the
composition of his table-ends, each end made of two solid
pieces halved into each other, and braced at the top by a
third piece mortised into the two.   The change in direction
of the outer line of each support in its upper portion, the
inner line left plain, the outer line decorated with a little
carving, seems to me an original motive, and the ends of
the supports, too, that touch the floor, are well managed:
their curves are good, and they do not interfere with our feet.

this,—does not suffer by having its beauty interfered with by that of its neighbor. The sides of the upper portion of this *étagère* are filled in with an arrangement of sticks that makes one think of a cobweb.

Cut No. 36 has an elegance of its own, distinct from that of cut No. 35.

Chinese Étagère, with Cupboard.
No. 35.

Chinese Étagère, with modern English Sconce.
No. 36.

I think both these pieces are Chinese, though so far as the arrangement of the shelves is concerned, the Japanese are as fond of it as the Chinese themselves. The sconce, for candles, that hangs over this *étagère*, is of modern English make, the pattern beaten out of rather thin brass. These sconces look very pretty on festive occasions, particularly at Christmas time, with a few bits of holly stuck about the brass disk.

In our small New-York—or why not say our small American—rooms, since a large room is certainly the exception?—in our small American rooms we want to leave the floor as free as possible, and to put on the walls whatever can be conveniently given to their keeping. I have already shown one device, on page 130, for making use of the walls to accommodate what ordinarily would stand upon the floor. This was in the entry-way of the house; but the need of room is as often felt in the living-room, owing to the small size of our rooms of which I have just spoken. At Herter's and at Cottier's there are several pretty hanging shelves, or *étagères*, intended to meet this want. They sometimes have little cupboards below the shelves in which frail objects of curiosity, or beauty, or both in one, can be kept under lock and key.

This clearing of the floor, and so making up somewhat for the scrimped rooms we most of us have to live in, is a point of no little importance in relation to comfort, and yet it is one we seldom give much thought to. The tendency is to crowd our rooms beyond their capacity, by which we make ourselves very uncomfortable, and destroy the value, as decoration, of many pieces, and their real usefulness as articles of furniture. What with easels, chairs not meant for use, little teetery stands, pedestals, and the rest of the supernumerary family filling up the room left by the solid and supposed useful pieces, it is sometimes a considerable

test of one's dexterity and presence of mind to make one's way from end to end of a long New-York drawing-room. Mignon's egg-dance was as nothing to it. In such

Much in Little Space.
No. 40.

perhaps, puzzled   ; he would have wondered what incident in the goddess's story could have given him an excuse

"To twitch the nymph's last garment off."

As I take it, Minerva has disrobed for the contest of beauty,

Hardly any piece of furniture is more troublesome to bring into harmony with the conditions of our modern room than the book-case. And one may well despair of bringing any help to those who are puzzling themselves

"What do you read, my lady?"
No. 54.

over the problem. If a man be a large student and a great accumulator of books, necessity solves the problem for him. He takes a room to himself, lines the walls with shelves, and covers all his available space with books. But that is not our problem. We want to have our books in our living-room, and we want pictures, and "objects," and

furniture, and comfort too. We want our books, not necessarily as Leigh Hunt said he liked his, "where he could
lean his head against them," but in close companionship,
and where we can get at them easily, and where we shall
be often tempted to get at them.

Cut No. 54 shows how this difficulty may be met in
one case, and it is a way that is by no means the invention of the owner of this particular book-case, but one that
has found favor with many another lover of books. The
present example was made to fit into a certain room where
it was fondly hoped it would remain for a half-dozen May-
days or so at the least. But it has since found itself at home
in two other rooms, and, on the whole, shows itself a man-
of-the-world in accommodating itself to what it finds at
hand. It is made of plain white pine, brought to a good
surface and shellacked, and its third year finds it with a
most beautiful color, only distinguishable from satin-wood
by a richer tone. It is twelve feet six inches long, the top
and bottom being each one piece, and it is about three
feet high. The bottom of the lowest shelf is four inches
from the floor, and the ends run up nearly five inches
above the top, and are connected by a strip at the back
of the same height. This makes a low wall of protection
for whatever may be set upon the top of the book-case,
and "finishes" it, as the slang phrase is, at once usefully
and handsomely. This book-case is divided into four by
three upright partitions, on each side of which slots are
sunk for the ends of the shelves to rest in, these shelves
being plain boards, all of the same thickness, of course,

Before leaving the living-room, I must allow myself the pleasure of a tilt against pianos as we make them in this the present year of grace—"bow-legged megatheriums," as somebody has hit them off, the ugliest pieces of furniture which we of this generation, fertile in ugliness, have as yet succeeded in inventing. The first pianos were prettier than any that have been made since, but they were too spindle-legged for real beauty, and owed too much to the color of the wood they were made of, with its pretty inlayings and marquetry, and painted panels above the key-board— too little to the excellence of their form. A handsome piano, one that an artist could enjoy the sight of, does not exist to-day out of museums, nor is made by any one of the legion of manufacturers. But a piano, even a "square" or a "grand," might be made a stately ornament to our drawing-rooms, and even the "uprights," which try to be as ugly as their four-footed and hooved brethren, but cannot wholly succeed, might be made much better than they are, in artistic hands. Some time ago there was on exhibition at Goupil's rooms, in New-York, a water-color drawing by one of the new school of Italian artists, Rossi, in which a lady was seated at a piano, in the style of Louis XIV., very ornate with flourishing, carving and gilding not exactly to be recommended, and having painted on the inside of the lid a dance of Cupids, or some sacred mystery of that sort. Why can't some of our young artists induce some one of the young piano-makers with his fortune to make, to combine with some clever designer, and devise a case for them to paint? The result might be delightful, and even if the first go-off were not wholly successful, it would show the way. It would be good to see a herd of the heavy-footed antediluvians that stretch their huge bulks about our drawing-rooms, turned out of their luxurious quarters, to give place to something that should seem more like an instrument of music. As it is, the loveliest woman that sits down to play at a modern piano is a little dimmed; the instrument, instead of setting off her beauty, seems to be doing its best to disparage it.

Attempts have been made by English designers to improve the shape of the modern piano-forte, but, thus far, they have only succeeded in adding to clumsiness of shape clumsiness of ornament. I wish some one would try the experiment of a perfectly plain case, and let it be decorated with color simply, after the fashion of the clavichord in cut No. 10. This rests upon a stand, and the raised lid has a pastoral landscape with figures painted inside.

CHAPTER III.

THE DINING-ROOM.

THE suggestion made early in these pages, that, in general, there is no need for a separate parlor, but that one room, the living-room, may be easily and comfortably made to serve all the social needs of the family,—a place of meeting for themselves, and a place in which to receive the visits of their friends,—was not meant to include the dining-room. There ought always, if possible, to be a separate room for meals, though I have known cases in plenty where there was no distinction between the dining-room and the living-room. But in all these cases the living-room was an exceptionally large apartment, and no confusion resulted, as is apt to be the case where the experiment is tried, from the appearance of Betty at the door with the announcement, "Please ma'am, I want to set the table, ma'am." As a rule, our rooms, especially in our cities, are too small to make this double employment possible, or at least convenient, and, as provision is almost always made for a separate dining-room in our houses, we may as well accept the arrangement as being, on the whole, the better one, considering the complicated ways of modern life. I wish we had not twisted and bound ourselves up so inextricably in these complicated ways. More than we think, or are willing to allow, of the difficulty that surrounds housekeeping in America,—the trouble with servants that makes such a mean tragedy in so many women's lives,—comes from the labor imposed upon the servants and upon the employers by the unnecessary fuss we make about living. The root of the difficulty is in the separation between our two lives, the domestic one and the social one, and the social one has been allowed to become so formal, ostentatious, and exacting, that in too many families it is by far the more important of the two—it regulates and controls the domestic life. It is hardly possible to dispute the proposition: that if the domestic life were made the leading one in any family, that is, if the whole household order, and all the arrangement and furnishing of the house, were made to accommodate and develop the family life,—the social element being obliged to suit itself to the family arrangement, and take them just as it found them,— life would be tenfold easier and tenfold happier than it is.

"Unless the kettle boiling be."
No. 65.

I know a private house where there is a table twelve feet long, at least,—fifteen, perhaps,—which is a spacious field for the deploying of all the household forces. It is a noble table, after a Jacobean model, and the cloth is often laid at one end of it, and dinner served without obliging those who have been working along its generous length to strike their tents and retreat with bag and baggage, or scrip and scrippage. This, however, would not be good to do as an every-day thing. One advantage in having a dining-room separate from the living-room is, that we get variety, and unbend the too stiff-stretched cord of daily work. This change of scene is almost a necessity to those who have been housed all day. But in this particular case, it was only a possibility that a part of the table might have been in use before the dinner, and that the worker's implements remained undisturbed during the meal. The big room in which the table stood was little used during the day, and it was only at night that it became the great center of the family gathering. And, certainly, it was a pleasant rallying-ground, and the scene of much hospitable intercourse and cheer. Our hostess knew the liking most people have for a cozy seclusion, and, if there were but few of us, she made a screen of ivy, against which brighter hues of leaf or flower were relieved, and so fenced off the "howling wilderness," as B. once called the rest of the table, until dessert came, which, after a turn about the room to inspect M.'s cabinet of *curios*, or a stroll in the garden, we came back to find, perhaps, served at the other end of the table.

We have such a treacherous climate in our northern states that it is useless to recommend a steady dining out-of-doors in summer-time, as is so often practiced in Middle France and in Southern Europe.   Still I have known a family to keep a table standing on the broad veranda of their country house, where they breakfasted, dined, and took supper every day in the summer-time that the weather permitted; and it was a very cheerful custom.   I think all the freedom we can get in our eating and drinking is desirable—all, I mean, that is consistent with comfort.   I wish even punctuality were not so much insisted on.   There ought to be a fixed hour, and then I would have all who are on hand sit down; but it ought not to be counted the mortal sin it is to come a quarter of an hour late, and it would n't be such a sin, if we did not make such formal affairs of our dinners.   There is one pleasant table around which as good company gathers as at any in the land, and there is form and ceremony enough to keep the wheels oiled; but if a straggler comes late, he neither gets cold soup nor the cold shoulder, but his excuse is accepted without too much examination, and perhaps he finds comfort in the fact that somebody else for whom he has a great liking is very apt to turn up even later than he.   It may cheer up some people who are made melancholy by thinking what delightfully disorderly times they seem fated to have at their own table, while at other people's houses everything is so quiet and respectable, to read the account Allan Cunningham quotes of the way things went on at Sir Joshua Reynolds's dinner-table:

The "Last Sweet Thing" in Corners.
No. 67.

The dining-table, the chairs and a sideboard are all the pieces we must have, and with these the room must be a small one if it is uncomfortably crowded.

Small or large, however, the dining-room ought to be a cheerful, bright-looking room. The east is a good aspect for it; a south-east aspect, if possible, because it is particularly pleasant to have the morning sun at breakfast, and then the southern sun makes the room cheerful all day, and plants will flourish too, and they are a happy addition to a dining-room, both for health and beauty. At dinner-time, if the dinner-hour be a late one, the aspect of the room will be of less importance, because the lamps will be lighted; but I think we shall find our account in having the morning sun strike across our breakfast-table.

The breakfast-table, however, as we have established it, following the English, I suppose, is an institution I wish were upset. Most people, if they would speak out their honest minds, would, I am sure, agree with me in thinking the American breakfast a mistake in our social economy. To force all the members of a family to get up and be dressed at a certain hour is not sensible, and yet a worse feature is, that they are all to sit down together at a common table, most of them in a very unregenerate state of mind, and not at all themselves, and in a condition far from suited to make social intercourse easy. The whole household is tormented to produce this unsatisfactory result. The servants have to get up at unnatural hours, and, in consequence, they are in a ticklish state of temper, ready for explosion on the most delicate expostulation. Nothing is ever well cooked, but this matters the less because nobody has any appetite. The business man—I mean the ideal business man—is occupied at breakfast-table with trying to do three things at once—to bolt his food, to bolt his newspaper, and to keep a steady eye on the clock. The only one of the three he succeeds in accomplishing is the last; he knows at every mouthful what time it is to a second, and he prances away from the table to catch his horse-car, steam-car, or ferry, every morning with the regularity of a planet. The servants have been routed out of bed; the wife, which is of vastly more importance, has been robbed of her morning rest; the children have been made uncomfortable,—all for no better end than to comply with a cast-iron system that never had any reason in it. Suppose the early breakfast-table were abolished, and let the separate members of the family take what light snack they wanted, when and where they would, those at home meeting later in the day,—say at noon,—for a regular breakfast, and the husbands and sons looking out for themselves at restaurants and cafés near their places of business. In Paris, gentlemen come home to breakfast, business people (the city being so built that it radiates from a center out) living as near to their shops and offices as they can contrive, so that the breakfast is generally a family meeting, and a very happy and cheerful one too. The various members of the family have got well shaken up by eleven or twelve o'clock, something has been accomplished, life has gone on more smoothly and equably, and parents and children are in a less critical and exasperating mood.

I don't mean to advocate a wild license in the matter
of lying a-bed, or getting up when you please.   But early
rising, or rising when it is time to rise,—for there never

"The pippins and cheese have come."
No. 68.

was a greater humbug than the doctrine of early rising for
its own sake,—is one thing, and early breakfasting for the
family in common is another.   Nobody needs (except day
laborers) much solid food immediately on rising, or after
being dressed.   A cup of coffee, a roll and butter, possibly

an egg—this would be enough and plenty for the average of people who live by their brains to work on till twelve o'clock.

"In tea-cup time of hood and hoop."
No. 69.

Another cut, No. 68, represents a more elaborate table,—more elaborate in its mechanism, though the design is every bit as simple. This table has an extension top, but the support of the top—the four legs and the frame-work—is solid. The top draws apart, and either a broad or a narrow leaf is inserted in the opening, according to the room wanted. At its largest, it will seat eight people comfortably,—one at each end, and three on each side,—and this is a large company!

How to light our dining-tables is often a puzzle, especially in the country.   It seems to me that, as a general
thing, our gas-fixtures are too heavy-looking, they pretend
to be too much.   I know none of them are really as heavy
or as solid as they look, but that does not make the matter better.   If they are not as heavy as they seem, there
is no use in their seeming heavier than they are!   If we

"Sweetness and Light."   Electrotype copy of a Silver Chandelier from Knole.
No. 70.

think about it, we shall perceive that there is no reason to
be given for a chandelier or a gaselier either being or
looking heavy or very solid.   Light is not heavy in itself,
nor are candles very heavy, while gas is, of course, a synonym for lightness.

The chandeliers and branches of old times were, as
everybody knows, models of delicacy and grace.   The aim
seemed to be to make the supports and holders of the

candles as harmonious with their whiteness and slenderness, and with the spiritual beauty of the light they were to give, as was possible. The slender arms that held the candles were wreathed and twisted into strong but graceful scrolls, and the main stem was made as slim as was consistent with the weight it had to bear—the base alone was loaded to prevent upsetting. It was a great deprivation when we were obliged to give up candles for illuminating. Nothing could be prettier than the effect of a room prepared for an evening party, decorated with flowers and lighted with wax candles. Candle-light is the only artificial light by which beauty shows all its beauty—it even makes the plain less plain. I do not know why it was that when gas came into use it was thought necessary to make all the chandeliers and branches clumsy and mechanical. Perhaps there was an unconscious connection in the manufacturers' minds between these instruments of illumination and the ponderous machinery and manipulation by which the gas is produced.

But, in reality, though nothing that may be devised for lighting our rooms can ever be so pretty to look at as candles, yet gas has also its poetry, and, as its use is established, we are bound to think how it may be used gracefully. There is no doubt that we Americans are unreasonably in love with machinery and contrivance, and that the makers of gas-fixtures have played upon our love of ingenuity until they have made us accept the most monstrous and complicated gas-machines for the decoration of our rooms. I live in the blessed hope that gas will one day be superseded by something better. It is unhealthy, it is troublesome, it is expensive, it tarnishes our silver, our picture-frames and our wall-papers, and how can it do this without injuring those who breathe it? But such as it is, we need not make it more disagreeable to the eyes and mind by bringing it into the parlor through a clumsy machine made up of wire tackle, hoisters, chains, weights and bronze frame-work. No more do we want statuettes or intricate ornaments upon our gaseliers. Beauty and utility are served best by a combination in shining metal (˙not in dull bronze) of carved and twisted branches through which the fluent gas shall really make its way, and that shall look as if the designer had taken into consideration the nature of the substance that was to pass through his pipes. At present, nearly all the designs for gas-fixtures appear directly to contradict the use they are to be put to, and instead of flowing, graceful lines, all the lines employed are angular and hard.

The best gas that is made nowadays is so poor, and so much trouble with the eyes is ascribed to its action (I wish the doctors would pound away as vigorously against gas and furnaces as it is their fashion to do against bad sewerage), that many people have learned to use either the German student-lamp or the French moderator, while some, more radical still, have frankly gone back to candles, and work only by them. With one of their lights and a soft coal fire, it is still possible to make one's parlor look as if it were a living-room and not a dying-room. Even if it be urged that a gas chandelier is the best means of illuminating a dining or supper table, because it permits all the people to see one another, I still demur that if elegance or picturesqueness is aimed at, the old silver-plated branches for candles are our only wear. Or such a chandelier as is shown in cut No. 70,—one of the pieces of a suite of bedroom furniture, toilet-table, mirror-frame, etc., etc., made out of solid silver, and still existing at Knole. Copies of this chandelier can be purchased. One of them was at Philadelphia, exhibited by Elkington. The expense of candles is an item hardly worth considering (it was not their dearness, but the troublesomeness of them that sent them out of use), and every woman knows that no light sets off her complexion, her dress, her ornaments, like the soft light of candles. The diamond, for example, is a dull stone by gas-light; its prismatic sparkle is only seen by candle-light.

Another modern tendency that seems to have nearly run the length of its tether is toward what is generally spoken of as *massive* furniture. We have been making our furniture so heavy of late, that the amount of solid wood in it added to the carving, inlaying, and veneering with different woods, has made it very expensive. Of course, the Bowery and Canal street have followed Broadway and the Fifth avenue, and we can hardly tell cheap furniture from dear, by the price. The so-called " East-lake" furniture has had much to do with keeping up the tendency we speak of. The one thing the designers of it seem to be after is to make it look "solid," and the one thing they seem in "mortal" dread of is that it shall be

graceful or elegant.   Some of the productions of the mills
that turn out this uncomfortable lumber are wonderful to
behold.   Most of it would look clumsy in an Italian palace.
In our American parlors and bedrooms it is not at home.
Many persons, however, who do not like it in a parlor
think it is just the thing for a dining-room.   Why we
should consider that the furniture of the dining-room ought
to be so much heavier than that of the parlor, I do not
know.   Probably we got it from the English, who, a few
years ago, had that notion, though they did not always
have it, as may be seen by cut No. 69.   This is copied
from a sideboard now in this country, and which many of
my readers will recognize as belonging to a style of which
many examples—some as elegant no doubt as this, some
very plain and inferior to it in design—are still to be
found in old houses.   In making this furniture, our ancestors
were aiming at lightness of form, economy of space and
delicacy of execution.   All the best pieces are finished with
extreme care, and they are so well put together—so skillfully and so conscientiously—as in many cases to have
defied the wear and tear of nearly a century.   Some chairs
which had, no doubt, been made by one of the best
English makers of the last century were recently bought
from the kitchen of a dismantled house (to which room
they had descended from the parlor, in the course of the
gradual ruin of the family), and though they had been put
by the beggarly inmates to the roughest use, and had lost
their seats, sacking, stuffing, covering and all, they needed
nothing but to have this lack supplied, and to be well

cleaned and polished, to be as good as ever they were.
It needs little examination to be assured that much of the
solidest-looking "Eastlake" furniture (I mean that made in

The Children's Quarter of an Hour.
No. 71.

this country) would have succumbed under the ungentle
treatment received by these chairs.

The "Eastlake" furniture must not, however, be judged
by what is made in this country, and sold under that name.
I have seen very few pieces of this that were either well
designed or well made. None of the cheaper sort is ever

either.   Mr. Herter has had some pieces made which were
both well designed and thoroughly well made, as all his
furniture is, however we may sometimes quarrel with his
over-ornamentation ; and Mr. Marcotte has also shown us
some good examples in this style.   But these are not to be
referred to as examples of cheapness, which was one of the
recommendations of the "Eastlake" furniture.   They are
only referred to as doing the style (if it be a style) more
justice than the lumps of things we see in certain shops,
though, in truth, these lumps are a good deal more like
the things recommended in Mr. Eastlake's book than the
stylish, elegant pieces designed by Messrs. Herter and
Marcotte.

The sideboard shown in cut No. 71, made by Cottier &
Co. from their own designs, is one of the best modern
sideboards I have seen, and well deserves to be recommended as a model.   It is made of hard wood, stained
black and then polished.   The drawers and doors have
key-plates and handles of brass, of that fine gold-color
which is now given to it, but, with only this exception,
there is nothing added to relieve the black of the wood-
work.   It will be observed that there is no carving, and
scarcely any molding on this piece ; but no one would
think anything wanting who should see it with even so
little upon it as a dish of fruit, a few glasses and water-
bottles, and on the shelf some blue plates, not put there
for show, but in daily use.   Much less would the eruptive
carving, and the stuck-on ornaments, and the coarse moldings that are considered indispensable to a "stylish" side-

board, be missed from this one on a feast day, when fruit and flowers, and glass, and silver, are busy "making reflections" on the gleaming surface for the benefit of those who have eyes!

The old-fashioned sideboards are often desirable pieces to have, but I do not believe in copying them, however skillfully it may be done. I would not hesitate, if I were in want of a sideboard, to buy a good example of the style shown in cut No. 69, if I could find a genuine old piece in first-rate condition, like some Mr. Sypher has recently picked up, and which are in his show-room. They are not such perfect specimens as the one which Mr. Lathrop has drawn, but they are of the better class, and one of them is an uncommon one to be on sale.

But unless I could get an old one, and a good one too, I should much prefer having one made after a design of my own time, to having a copy made of something old-fashioned. We make pretty things nowadays, or can make them, and the difficulty of getting things simple and unpretending in design is not half so great as we pretend to believe. The trouble, half the time, is with ourselves. We don't want things simple and unpretending; I mean, very few of us do. We are not strong enough in our own taste to be able to relish plain surfaces without panels, edges without moldings, and a pleasingness, generally, that depends wholly on good proportions and nice finish. Ornament is a thing to be desired, but to be desired it must be good, and it must be in its place. If the reader be a young married couple, let him look up from this page with candid eyes at the set of "Eastlake" furniture which she has just bought with the money he has been saving up for a year or two for that especial purpose, and ask herself how much of the ornament that is stuck upon it or gouged out of it, regardless of cheapness, is good. And, ten to one, if he can find a bit of it that is good, it will be put on in the wrong place,—that is, where it cannot be seen.

Cut No. 72 is a more homespun sideboard, but a useful one, and far from ill-looking. It is a genuine old Puritan piece, one found in a barn-yard, where it had for many years been given over to the hens. From having cold chicken on its top, it had come to have warm chicken inside, and it was no easy matter to remove the traces of the hens' housekeeping. But solid oak, well pinned together and mortised, is proof against much ill-usage and

Cut No. 75 is a group of pieces of furniture, all of it belonging to Old Colony times, drawn by Mr. Lathrop for Bryant & Gay's "History of the United States." The

Old Colony Days.
No. 75.

cupboard at the left belongs to the same class, and I think to the same time, as the one which was figured on page 168, cut No. 72. These pieces were made of oak, and are fastened together by wooden pins. The carving, though rude, is effective. There is not much of it, but it is put where it does the most good. A desire to get something of the effect of carving in relieving plain surfaces, without at the same time incurring much expense, explains the device of pieces of turned-work, cut in halves, and fastened by the flat side to certain parts of the piece, as at the ends of the division between the upper and lower baluster columns, and between the lower baluster and the foot on which the piece rests. These are best seen at the left-hand side. Similar pieces of turned-work, cut in two, are made to serve as pilasters, one at each side of the door, with a round-arched panel in the upper of the two stories into which the cupboard is divided. There is no waste room in this cupboard. Besides the six cupboards* proper, there are drawers in the three other divisions,—in that which answers to the frieze, in the base, and in the part between the upper and lower range of closets. The height of the whole is such that the top can easily be reached with the hand, and it is thus equivalent to a shelf. In this old piece, as in all of the same style that I have seen, color has been employed as a further orna-ment. The baluster columns were painted black, or red picked out with black, and the other turned ornaments as well, while the panels were occasionally decorated with ciphers in a flourish of heraldic foliage, or with birds and flowers in a half-conventional, half-natural style. But

---

* How the word cupboard has changed its meaning! From standing for a set of shelves (boards) on which plate could be displayed, it has come to be applied to a closet in which things can be shut up. Some of the old cupboards, like the sideboards in vogue to-day, had closets below them, and these have gradually usurped the name of what was once the superior portion.

these painted decorations have been in almost all cases effaced,—whether intentionally, or merely by hard usage, cannot be told. I wish they had been left, for I should like some examples of homely, but effective, color decoration to survive, and point the way to something better in the art of decorating furniture than prevails at present. I have already touched on this subject, but at that time I did not know that there was any one here who was likely to help us in getting the sort of decoration needed. The house-painters cannot help us, though there are men among them who could if they were made to see the profit of it; and our artists (being so superior, as they are to Giotto, Delli, Gentile da Fabrino, Paolo Uccello, and the rest of the early Italians, who all painted furniture, door-panels, bridal chests, trays, shields,* whenever they could get a chance)—our artists are, for the most part, above any such degradation of their profession, and it is only in England that we see a return to the charming old fashion. There it is, nowadays, getting to be common to call upon artists to do this work, and some interesting results have been produced. In the Philadelphia Exhibition there was a piece of furniture with panels painted by Mr. Murray. It was exhibited by Messrs. Collinson & Lock. The reason why we do not see more of these pieces painted by the

---

* We have several specimens of this work in our country: panels taken from these Italian chests in the Jarves collection in Yale College, and a fine example of a chest with its panels still in place in the Boston Museum of Fine Arts, with three or four trays in the Jarves collection, and in the little-known and neglected but most precious Bryan collection of pictures—early Italian and others—in our own city in the possession of the Historical Society.

old Italians is, that the panels have been cut out and framed as pictures, in the greed of amateurs and owners in the last hundred years. Some day, no doubt, the same fate will overtake this fine cabinet decorated by Mr. Murray. On page 145, cut No. 39, there was shown a cabinet made by Cottier & Co., for which Mr. Lathrop painted two most beautiful panels. And Mr. H. M. Lawrence, of Albany, beside having decorated a number of pieces of china in a very interesting way, has also painted several panels with flower-decoration that seem to me to show much promise. I wish somebody had venturesomeness enough to design a cupboard, or wardrobe, or book-closet for Mr. Lawrence or Mr. Lathrop to decorate; but in these matters, there seems nowadays not only to be no venturesomeness, but no desire to get out of the comfortable ruts we are all jogging along in.

Yet, all the time people are doing things to please themselves, and striking out in the experiment some good ideas. Thus a gentleman told me the other day that, wishing to fit up his kitchen in a substantial way, he seized the opportunity offered by the sale at a bargain of a considerable number of paneled outside shutters taken from an old house, and still in good condition, from having been made of hard wood, and in a time when carpenters knew what a panel meant; and with these he wainscoted his kitchen, paneling the walls at small expense, and making a stylish room of it. If people really loved their houses,—loved them as we *can* love material things from their association with what is nearest and dearest to us,—

and if they did love them, they would n't be so willing to give them up and change for new ones, as they are with us,—they would find many devices to improve them, not in the mere "dumb-waiter," "permanent wash-tub" sense of the word, but in the sense that makes them homes for home-loving, cultured families,—devices that, while they

Extension Dining-Table and Chairs.
No. 76.

would add much to their attractiveness, would make small demands upon the purse.

The difficulty of getting a dining-table that shall be both good-looking and serviceable has already been descanted upon in these pages, but, I fear, to little purpose. I give here a few illustrations that may help some of my readers to a solution. Cut No. 76 shows a table recently made by Cottier & Co., with its accompanying chairs. Cut No. 77 is a variation on the design for the end support of this same table. This particular table was made of oak, and with regular and systematic rubbing—five minutes or so each day, before the cloth is laid—it will acquire a mirror-like smoothness and polish. Now, a dining-table, as a rule, is seen only when it is in use, and then only the top of it; so that it may be made of two kinds of wood, one less expensive than the other, as was done in the case of the table shown in cut No. 68, page 158. As for costliness, the hard woods are all about the same, barring mahogany, which was dear before it came to be the fashion, and is dearer since, of course. But the pleasure that a good mahogany top to one's dining-table will give, as the years go by, is worth straining a point for; particularly as mahogany is a first-rate wood for wear, and literally, with good treatment, proves better and better as life wears away. The best combinations would be walnut and mahogany, or ash and oak; but the top ought, by rights, to be of one or the other of these two handsome hard woods,—oak or mahogany,—so that it may bear the taking the cloth off at dessert. Then, the rest of the table might be of some cheap wood. In cut No. 76, the frame of the table is shown to be very heavy and strong. There is no need of this, unless the table is a large one, and meant to stretch out on occasion to a great length, as was the case with this one. In such a table, all the folding-rack that supports the additional leaves has to be accommodated by sliding back under the ends, and the table must be solidly built to bear the weight and strain. Cut No. 77 shows a lighter structure: in the drawing, the size of the balls turned on the legs is a trifle exaggerated; they are, besides, rather egg-shaped than round. The bottom rail will be found a convenience, and not in the way. It will be noticed, too, that in both these tables the top projects well

Design for End Support of Dining-Table.
No. 77.

over the frame, so that there is no danger of knocking one's knees against the table-leg in sitting down. This should always be carefully looked out for in constructing a dining-table; to knock one's knees in sitting down to dinner is one of the minor miseries of life.

I have already spoken of the desirableness of introducing the fashion of decorating furniture with painting. I have recalled to my readers the commonness of painted decoration in early Italian times, when cabinets, sideboards, wardrobes and trays were painted with figure subjects,— religious, historical, mythological,—often by artists who afterward became famous. The peasant-furniture of Europe, particularly in Germany, Switzerland, the Tyrol, and Holland, is decorated, and often with pretty effect, with a mixture of a primitive arabesque design and flowers. And now and then one sees at Castle Garden an immigrant's wooden chest that, with its bright colors, shines among the shabby trunks and boxes of the rest of the company like a peacock among the barn-door fowl. In the Exhibition, too, we had an opportunity of seeing some of the coarsely painted but effective furniture from Tunis,—among the rest, some of the hanging shelves like the one on page 130, cut No. 3. All these shelves were early bespoke, and late in the Exhibition it was impossible to buy one, for people who could n't think such coarse carpentry and rough painting good enough for their parlors, saw that they would look very well in the half-light of their entries; and certainly few hat-racks and hall-mirrors at the fashionable shops are half so pretty as these rude articles.

Cut No. .78 is a copy of an engraving in M. Rodolphe Pfnor's "Ornamentation Usuelle," Paris, 1866–7, where it is described as manufactured at Toelz, Tyrol, Bavaria. The material is of pine, perhaps, and the decoration is painted,— flowers and their leaves, with borders, bands, and ornaments in lively colors on a yellow ground. The back of the chair, which is in the same style, is pierced at one point in a heart-shape, but the remaining surface is covered with a painted decoration. The tops of these tables are often a slab of slate. A continuous foot-rail runs around the four sides, so near to the floor that the foot easily slides upon it without much thinking; and, although the legs have a strong outward slant, the top projects so well that they are not in the way. A drawer slides in grooved pieces fastened to the under side of the table-top, and is handy for holding the table-cloth and napkins. A few

Table and Chair from Tyrol, Bavaria.
No. 78.

years ago, Messrs. Kimbel & Cabus made several tables after a design similar to this, but they were decorated with carving rather than painting, and this made them more costly. I remember, however, that they were very pretty, and seemed all the prettier for breaking up the monotony of New-York furniture shops with something altogether new on this side the water.

as ours are poor, and we go on robbing them without in
the least diminishing the supply.   In France, in Germany
and in Italy, the workmen have attained great skill in
reproducing the design of the Renaissance time, but this is
mere copyism; when they attempt to originate, they are,
artistically, little above London or New-York.

We have, therefore, in our poverty of the artistic faculty,
thrown ourselves on bareness or simplicity, as we like to
call it, and, in default of the power to carve and to produce luxuriant forms, we have covered up our nakedness
with a world of bric-à-brac.   For closed cabinets, rich in
architectural forms and sculptures, caryatides and panels, we
have *étagères,*—mere assemblages of shelves, with no beauty
in themselves, and meant to pass unnoticed in the beauty
or curiousness of the multitude of objects that fill them.
We make no more tapestry, and we try to persuade ourselves that wall-paper can take the place of that mode of
decoration with its entertaining individuality.   We have but
little art in our day that would have been called art in the
great days; and, in our own country, hardly any art at all
that is reckoned such outside of our own boundaries.   At
any rate, if the statement be quarreled with, we must
admit that we have no painting or sculpture that can fairly
be called "decorative," and we never shall have until our
artists get down from their high-horses and condescend
("condescend!"— hear the word, spirits of Giotto and
Raphael, of Veronese, and Titian, and Tintoret!) to paint
our walls for us, nor think it enough to sell us their little
squares of paint at killing prices—the frames not included!

CHAPTER IV.

THE BEDROOM.

"BLESSINGS," said Sancho, "on the man who invented sleep!
It wraps a man all about like a blanket!"

So FAR as possible, all the rooms in this ideal house of ours
front the sun, or are visited by the sun for an hour or
two every day. I hold this almost essential to a bedroom,—
that it should have, not merely light and air, but the direct
rays of the sun, and that there should be no furniture nor
hangings in the room that are likely to be injured by the
sun. It is not always possible in New-York City to obtain
this southern exposure. Owing to her position, and to the
direction which as a consequence of that position has been
given to her streets, it so happens that, with the exception
of those which are built upon the avenues, all the houses
have one side always in shade, and the other always in sun.
And as the lots present their ends, not their breadth, to the
street, the bedrooms have to be divided, so that one half
have a northern, and the other half a southern exposure.
The houses on the avenues facing east and west get the

sun in the morning and afternoon, but none during the
day; so that we are all about in the same box. But
everybody who has had any experience of a New-York

A Duchesse.
No. 81.

winter knows that the sunny rooms are the pleasantest,
and I think we all have a feeling that they are the
healthiest.

Everybody who has lived in Paris, or anywhere in Europe, knows the prejudice that exists there against admitting the night air into bedrooms. The German horror of fresh air inside the house at any time, whether by night or day, is well known, and has been harped on by travelers—English and American—for many a long year; but,

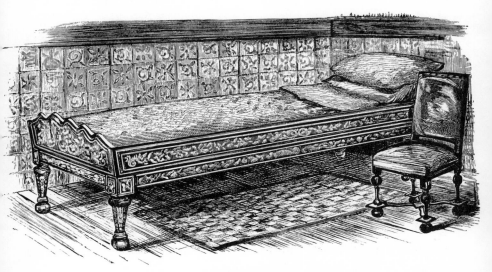

Dutch Bedstead.
No. 82.

in France and Italy, the prejudice is chiefly directed against fresh air at night. In Paris, educated people will gravely tell you that you will become blind if you leave your windows open at night; and if, after a year of the deadly practice, you ask them how they account for your eyes being still unimpaired, they only shrug their shoulders and insist that Americans and English are not like other human beings. For my part, I like as much sun and air as I can

get, and should never be able to sleep at all if I must
have my window shut at night, while, at the same time,
I admit that the Germans, French and Italians are as
healthy as any other people, and get along famously under
a system that I am persuaded would soon make an end
of me.

The doctrine I am now stating, then, so far as it is
doctrine at all, is to be considered as only my own affair,
and to have no authority behind it except myself and a
few hundred physicians, English and American, who would
confess, I dare say, if put upon their honor, that plenty of
sunlight, fresh air,—night and day,—open fires, the absence
of furnaces, and also of drain-pipes and gas, would make
their own skill little necessary in the preservation of health,
and diminish greatly the amount of disease to be cured.

But whether or not we can get all these advantages
extended over the whole house, I am sure it would be a
good thing to secure them for our bedrooms. Besides
exposure to the sun during the day, there should be some
means of letting in the outside air at night. If people
object to bluntly opening a window, then some one of
those ventilators that are attached to the window-frame
may be used; or, better, it may be ventilated by a good
open fire-place, which ought to be the only means of heating a bedroom, as indeed it is the cheerfulest and most
attractive. Now that soft coal is so abundant, of many
sorts, from the English cannel to the American kinds, and
that grates for burning it are common enough, there is no
excuse for using anthracite, either in a grate or stove.

Cut No. 85 was designed by Mr. John Miller, and was
made by Mr. Matthias Miller. It is made of oak. The
side-rails pass through the corner-posts, and are held by
the wooden pins, the ends of which are seen projecting

from the sides of the posts which are in shadow. The
three rails of the ends—one at the top below the carved
finials, and the two others near the bottom—also pass

"A bed is the most delightful retreat known to man."
No. 86.

through the corner-posts. The upright pieces that make
the upper division of the foot-board are cut out in a pattern where the edges come together. The answering pieces
in the head-board are left plain with closed joints; but the
top of each piece is cut into a pattern, and the assemblage

not too daring, or when the makers are content with copying the quieter Eastern patterns, are a great improvement on the older manufactures. But one may as well spend his money for an Eastern carpet outright as buy one of these English carpets. There would be the certainty of getting a design that had no taint of South Kensington in it, and that would be sure not to be the same through any square foot of its space. For one thing, Eastern art is valuable to us: it rebukes at every turn our scientific love of precision and symmetry, shows us the charm of irregularity, and teaches us how to make two sides of a thing alike while keeping them quite different. Whether we shall ever get this into our blood, I don't know. It is an essential principle of all the best decorative art; and necessarily so, because all such design is as far removed as possible from mechanical assistance, and has no other rule or measure than the eye acting through the hand. No two Ionic capitals of Greek workmanship, even in the same temple, are alike in anything except general size and character. No more are any two Doric caps alike, nor any two moldings of any style, nor any two successive feet of any Greek ornament. The notion instilled into our minds that the Greek architecture is all monotony and repetition is of English or German origin.

There needs to-day to be a protest made by some one against the mechanical character of our decoration, for, with an unexampled demand for decoration in our furniture, our furnishing, our jewelry, our porcelain, there has come an unexampled supply, and the manufacturers, of

course, bring all the labor-saving appliances they can contrive to supply this demand.　Immense furniture-mills are
set up, and to such perfection has machinery attained, that
the logs go in at one door, and come out at another fash-

"When clothes are taken from a chest of sweets."
No. 88.

ioned in that remarkable style known here as "Eastlake,"
and which has become so much the fashion that grace and
elegance are in danger of being *taboo* before long.　Then
"rugs" being all the rage, and the beautiful ones being,
as they always must be, expensive, the manufacturers are
turning out cheap rugs by the acre, which are no whit

better—nay, are much worse—than the carpets of thirty or forty years ago. So with pottery and porcelain,—our china-shops are filled with things whose only recommendation to our novelty-loving people is their novelty and their loudness. And all these things—the furniture, the rugs, the pottery—are so cheap, that everybody gets them, and, of the smaller decorative things, gets so many that our homes are overrun with things, encumbered with useless ugliness, and made to look more like museums or warerooms than like homes of thinking people and people of taste.

I dare say, however, that all this superabundance—superabundance in the supply and superabundance in the buying—is necessary, and that not only good to trade and to manufacture, but good to art and taste, will come out of it. The way of it will be something like this: Exclusiveness being natural to human beings (it comes simply and excusably enough from our dislike of monotony and of repetition), people will demand more than they do now things that show some individuality in design, that are not made "in quantities to suit purchasers,"—that are not even to be had in pairs. Then we shall find the makers of furniture producing single pieces or single sets, into which the workman has put some special design which he does not copy in the next piece, even if he keep the general form. Design, and finish, and serviceableness, will be most considered, and cheap display—the bane of almost all our fashionable furniture nowadays—will be avoided. When a few rich people, who have an educated taste besides, will

encourage the production of furniture that is worth admir-
ing and keeping for its own sake, not merely because it is
in the fashion, we shall see the turn of the tide. At present, there is hardly anything at all of this done even by
the richest people (I mean, little that I hear of); and as
for the general run of us, we don't so much as think of
doing it. People naturally and reasonably count the cost,
and when they find that it not only costs a good deal of
money but a good deal of time and study to get a piece
of furniture well designed, they just wont try to do it, and
fare as well as they can without.

At present, then, we are in this strait. The things we see
for sale in the shops are all either good or bad or indifferent
copies of old-fashioned things, or of Oriental things of to-
day. Hardly anything with the stamp of our own time
and country is to be had. What, then, are the young
people to do who want to furnish their houses, and have
comparatively little, or really little, money to do it with?
I say in the first place, that there is no excuse nowadays
for anybody having ugly things. If they have them, they
are themselves to blame, for they must have chosen ugliness and rejected, if not beauty and elegance, then simplicity. "Wedding presents," I hear some reader whisper.
Yes, I know. But wedding presents are almost always of
silver, or ornaments, or small things that after a year's
display where they can catch the giver's eye on reception
days and "calls," can be stowed away. Few people are
cruel enough to send in furniture; for that the young
housekeepers are responsible.

For myself, I have such a dislike to almost the whole of what are called in housekeeping "modern improvements" (being a disbeliever in the benefits of gas, plumbing, and heating apparatus, except where, as in hotels and factories, they are necessary on a grand scale), that I naturally prefer a contrivance like the "cistern," cut No. 95,—convenient, pretty to look at, and in no danger of becoming a diphtheria-trap,—to one of our fixed basins. Another, the reader may remember, was shown on page 127 . However, I am well aware that there is a sufficient reason for our American wholesale adoption of mechanical contrivances in the miserably inefficient character of our servants. In nine cases out of ten, we use gas, furnaces and plumbing instead of lamps or candles, open fires and movable washing-apparatus, because it saves immensely in the labor and expense necessary to carry on a household. But, nowadays, when better servants are to be had, and "service" is getting to be more and more a profession, we may reasonably plead for a more domestic, and a less hotel and steam-boaty, way of living, knowing that in doing so we are pleading also for healthier ways of living, and not merely for picturesqueness. Besides, it may cheer up the weaker brethren who are made uncomfortable by doing differently from their neighbors, to know that a great many people are on the side of reform in this matter, and that it may almost be said to be "the fashion" (magical word!) nowadays to work by a "student-lamp," or a "moderator,"—the perfection of light-givers,—with an open fire of soft coal in the grate, and no pestilent, life-destroying furnace within the four walls; while, upstairs, the plumbing is confined to the bath-room, the movable wash-stand with its china and glass and "comforts" generally, being restored to its old supremacy,— taken out of its closet prison, and set in light and air.

A Place for Everything.
No. 95.

We will waste no words with people who go through England, with its absolute perfection in the art of domestic living, and whose good inns everywhere, in town or country, make our bare, dreary barracks more desolate in the remembering—and sigh for what they call the "modern improvements" they have left behind them. To some people, a great ingredient in the charm of Europe is, that they are rid of the very things that others are all the time sighing for.

A friend writes: "I shall never forget, when remembering the minor pleasures of my visit to England, my first experience of an 'inn.'

"We went directly to Chester, and, to the disgust of the porters, declined to go where, being evidently 'gentry,' we should have gone by instinct—to the elegant spic-and-span, bran-new 'Grosvenor,' but insisted on being carried to one of the old-fashioned inns. We found a large house with its traditional 'landlady' in the bar, and were shown into a waiting-room while our parlor was made ready. This proved to be a large apartment, furnished in a comfortable, home-like way, with the same sort of furniture that would have been found in an ordinary English house—I mean, there was nothing in the room that suggested it had been furnished 'on contract.' When dinner-time came, we found the table laid in our own parlor, the waiter and his boy in black coats, white neck-cloths, and white cotton gloves, and the table set like one's own and different in no respect, not even in the quality of the furniture, from what one often saw afterward in England at the tables of very good people. We had ordered our dinner beforehand, the landlady having come up and asked us what we would like, very civilly, and kindly helping us to choose, so that when we sat down, the tiresome waiter we had left three thousand miles away, with his skipping alternations from freezing neglect to pushing obsequiousness, and his 'bill-er-fare' with its chaos come again, and its damnable iteration, were a forgotten nightmare, and the dinner was a foretaste of Paradise. I remember that after dinner when the dessert was set,—the cloth being actually removed and the old mahogany revealed,—the waiter, in putting on the table some handsome old Worcester plates (made in the days when there was a Worcester that had something better to do than making bad copies of Japanese perfections), whispered that 'Mrs. ——, thinking we might like, as Americans,

to see some old china, had sent these up,' and how was it
possible after that to feel that we were in a hotel? The
surprise was reserved, however, for bed-time, when, on
going to our chamber, we found a small fire flickering
cheerfully in the grate, the candles lighted, the curtains of
the four-post bedstead drawn and the clothes turned down,
while at one side of the room, placed upon a cloth of its
own and with its own towel-stand supplied with bath-towels,
was the welcome hat-bath, an English gift to the world
worth all the sewing-machines and steam-engines that were
ever invented. Here was a comfortable lap of fortune to
have fallen into, and we hummed with Dr. Johnson those
lines of Shenstone that no home-staying American (at least,
since the good old days of 'Bunkers!') can ever understand the sense of:

> ' Whoe'er has traveled life's dull round,
>   Where'er his stages may have been,
>   May sigh to think he still has found
>   The warmest welcome at an inn!'

"Among my reminiscences of travel, I do not know of
any sharper contrast than between this comfortable inn at
Chester and the hotel we went to on arriving in New-
York—one of the three or four 'first-class' hotels; for,
whereas in Europe no one who is merely after comfort,
and not after a showy way of spending money, ever goes
in a city to the first-class hotels, here at home it is never
safe to go to any other. At this hotel we were shown
into a big bare room, containing just what was necessary

for decent living—a carpet, a bed, a bureau, a looking-glass, a table and four chairs, with the inevitable furnace-hole in the wall, the gas-burner where no one could use it in dressing, and the wash-basin in the narrow closet—a scientific desolation (your room being exactly like every other in the caravansary) which we Americans have carried to perfection. At dinner, we sat in the well-lighted, handsomely proportioned dining-hall, and 'fed'* with the multitude—the gentleman in front of us enjoying his ice-cream, water-melons, peaches and coffee all at once—he at the tail of the *carte* while we were at the head. Yet for all this bare and bleak discomfort, we paid far more than for the English hospitality."

The lady's dressing-table, cut No. 99, also designed by Mr. Sandier, was engraved in Paris by M. Guillaumot. The table is low and long, and of good breadth, and has two drawers. The glass is large, and I believe does not swing. The shelves at the sides, supported on slender columns, are rather intended for lights than for the flower-glass and

---

* With what instinct in the choice of a word Shakspere makes Lady Macbeth betray her scorn for the people who flocked to her solemn supper. "*Feed*," she said, "*Feed*, and regard him not!" If she had been thinking of them as human beings, she would have said "Eat!" but she thought of them as swine, and her word fitted her thought. This remarkable woman, whose lady-like instincts make us the more regret her indiscretions, and more willing to excuse them on account of that neglected education which somebody beside ourselves has deplored, shows, in another passage of the same scene, that she had a genius for hospitality:

> "My royal lord,
> You do not give the cheer: the feast is sold
> That is not often vouch'd, while 't is a making,
> 'T is given with welcome: To *feed* were best at home;
> From thence, the sauce to meat is ceremony;
> Meeting were bare without it."—MACBETH, Act III, Scene 4.

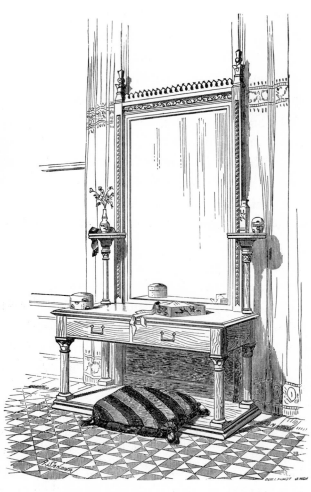

"And now confessed the toilet stands displayed."
No. 99.

knickknacks the reader sees. This seems to me a good
design, and one that might be easily copied. I think it
will look best in wood stained black and polished.

CHAPTER V.

WORDS HERE AND THERE.

A WEEK or two ago, at a prettily furnished table,

"In after dinner talk
Across the walnuts and the wine,"

chance brought up the name of a poet-philosopher very dear to some Americans who were young thirty years ago, never thought of without a stirring of the heart, mingled of reverence and affection. It seems that in his old age this man, like many another whose work has been a force to help lift his generation up to a higher plane, is not so rich in this world's goods as he would be if all the grateful thoughts that spring up at the mention of his name were coined into gold and poured into his lap. He lives in a plain, good house in the country, the windows of which look out upon a modest acre or two of his own; he eats plain fare, and is pleased with what he eats, and cares, no more than the most homespun of his neighbors, for luxuries, or for the things that go for show. His luxuries are

the liberal sunshine that streams in at his windows, the
Æolian harping of the pine-tree grove that shelters his
house, and the peace that dwells within its walls. It hap-
pened that some well-to-do people from the city had been
visiting the poet's family, and they brought back to town
a melancholy report of the condition of things they found
there. Would Peek-in street believe it! The poet's table
was set out with plain white china (Heaven grant that a
closer view might not have found it only earthenware!),
and some of it was chipped, and the tumblers were not
mates, and the wine-glasses were in such a way that they
actually had to be supported by the tumblers! It matters
not that to this plain house, and to its frugal New England
table, came the picked society of the world, or that the
best people in the land think it an added pleasure to their
lives to be of the company. These fine city people (one
wonders how they came there!) saw nothing but the plain
living, and found no compensation in the high thinking.

An incident like this might make one ashamed of the
time he has given to thinking and writing about "things,"
if he could not comfort himself with the assurance that
there has been nothing in his treatment of the subject, or
in the advice he has given, inconsistent with good sense
or with right ways of living. It has been taken for granted
that all his readers knew how little furniture, and decorations, and equipage, have to do with happiness or with
true largeness of life. Almost all the great men of this
world have lived in an absolute independence of things.
The shining lights of our own time especially have been,

To this tearful indictment, what can we reply? First, it is a fact that many of the things figured in these pages are inexpensive compared with things of the same general, decorative and elegant character that are to be found in the rich shops. Very many of them belong to people who are not at all rich in this world's goods; and in those that only exist in the drawings of Messrs. Babb, Inglis, and Sandier, the intention has been to make them as inexpensive as possible. I believe that where people have clubbed together and had four or five of any one of these pieces made by a country carpenter, they have found they got far more for their money than they could have got by going even to Canal street,—I mean that their handsome table or book-case has not cost them as much as a homely, ill-made travesty of the "style" would have cost them.

No doubt many of the designs are of costly pieces, far beyond the reach of any but long purses. But let the reader note that these pieces have always been selected by the writer on account of their elegance and good taste rather than for ornate richness and luxuriousness; and all through these pages the writer's aim has been to put before the reader what are believed to be good models, not with the expectation that they would be copied or imitated, nor often holding out the hope that their likes could be had again, but only with the hope that something might be accomplished in improving the general taste. Yet even of this the writer has said as little as possible, for it is no small presumption for any one to think he can help his fellows much, and he felt pretty sure that, before he got to the end of his task, he would find he needed help as much as any one.

There is a fortune in store for any one who to-day will supply the public with well-made, well-designed furniture— well-designed both for beauty and use—at cheap rates. It can be done by first getting from competent hands designs that have been thoroughly thought out, reduced to their simplest elements, and so planned that they can be made in quantities,— on the same principle that Canal street furniture is made, the difference being in the workmanship and in the design; for it is not only the fact that the Canal street stuff is made by the hundred dozen at a time that makes it cheap. It is because the wood is not seasoned, and because all the parts are put together in the least scientific, "good enough," way. Injustice is often done to what are called "expensive establishments" by our not knowing the cost of making their goods. A chair made by Herter or Marcotte is put together in such a way that only violence can break it; and it can be re-stuffed and re-covered for fifty years, and be as good as new. Now, almost all the furniture made by these houses is made to order; they keep very little material in stock, and even their chairs and sofas, of which they keep more ready-made than of the other regulation-pieces, have to be covered to suit individual tastes. Now, let the reader think what is implied in this "making to order." A staff of accomplished draughtsmen has to be employed, and an accomplished draughtsman, if he be a steady, facile workman, is always able to command a good salary. Then, the best workmen that are to be had are kept all the year round on good wages; and, lastly, only the best materials are used, and for covering and the like, the fashion must be not only kept pace with, but wealthy paying custom depends on its being also a little antedated. I do not speak now of rents and the salaries of employés, but merely of the necessary expenses of producing furniture. We must remember, too, that rich buyers do not want their orders repeated for other customers, nor do they want things that other people have; and to make one piece of furniture alone is more expensive than to make six pieces alike. Does a man whose shoes have to be made for him exclusively, so that every projecting joint shall live at ease on its own corner lot, expect to pay no more than the boy who can slip his well-shaped foot into the first shoe of his size that is presented .Writer

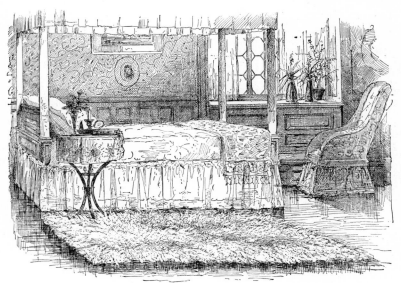

pleads in extenuation that he is really misunderstood, and that he does not mean any harm! He stands by all he has said about economy and simplicity, and the possibility of making our houses attractive without, at the same time, making ourselves uncomfortable by spending more money than we can afford in furnishing and decorating. But when it comes to giving illustrations that will support his propositions, he is met by a difficulty. Many of the pieces of furniture that in design and purpose answer to his notions are, in fact, expensive pieces. He takes them where he finds them, and has them copied as faithfully as he can, and without any attempt to show them less elegant and costly than they really are. But whoever will be at the pains to look over the pictures in this book of his will admit that, whatever the money goes for, it does not go for carving, and flourish, and display for display's sake. Nor is it a fact that all the things shown are expensive, that is, compared with the prices that would be paid for fashionable pieces of furniture intended for the same uses. One may well despair of getting anything cheap when he finds that even chairs so ostentatiously bare and matter-of-fact as those made by the Shakers, or the Vienna bentwood chairs, cost as much as some to be found in the fashionable shops that make a good deal more show. People are slow to learn, women especially, it would seem, that the reverse of the rule which holds true of their dresses is true of most of the furniture called fashionable nowadays.

Part III

Other Comments

on

Late Victorian Decor

by H. P. Spofford, R. Randall, Russell Lynes

Drawing-room in Modern Gothic.

A·Drawing·Room·Corner·

R.W. EDIS, F.S.A. ARCHT ❋

The Late Victorian American art critic Harriet P. Spofford (her *Art Decoration Applied to Furniture,* N.Y., 1877, will soon appear as a separate volume in our Library of Victorian Culture).

THE EASTLAKE.

SOMETHING more than half a dozen years ago, a number of essays, written by Mr. C. L. Eastlake, were printed in the various English publications, and afterward collected in a volume that has done a great work toward revolutionizing the manufactur? of furniture. Criticism, in the beginning, was almost altogether barred from the ideas propounded in these essays by Mr. Eastlake's asserting that if the virtuoso should find them wanting in antiquarian research, the scientific man in technical information, and the sentimentalist in the poetry of art, it must be remembered that nothing more had been attempted than to show readers how to furnish their houses picturesquely, yet with reference to modern ideas of comfort.

The book met a great want. Not a young marrying couple who read English were to be found without " Hints on Household Taste " in their hands, and all its dicta were accepted as gospel truths. They hung their pictures and their curtains just as Mr. Eastlake said they should; laid their carpets, colored their walls, hinged their doors, arranged their china, bought their candlesticks, insisted on their andirons, procured solid wood, abjured veneering, and eschewed curves, all after Mr. Eastlake's own heart. If, now, it is seen that some things which Mr. Eastlake laid down as immutable and irrevocable laws of art are really matters of taste, to be left to individual decision, it nevertheless remains true that the book occasioned a great awakening, questioning, and study in the matter of household furnishing. Presently there arose a demand for furniture in the " Eastlake style."

The upholsterers, with whom Mr. Eastlake had made quarrel in his pages, denied that there was any such style. Mr. Eastlake himself had said that he recommended the "readoption of no specific type of ancient furniture which is unsuited, whether in detail or in general design, to the habits of modern life." It was the spirit and principles of early manufacture which he desired to see revived, and not the absolute forms in which they found embodiment. The demand, however, was one which obliged the upholsterers to pocket their grudge, and if there were no Eastlake style, to invent one; for to-day Eastlake chairs, ugly past belief, but invincibly strong, Eastlake bedsteads, clean-shaped and charming, Eastlake wash-stands, dressing-cases, drawers, and cabinets, are to be seen everywhere disputing the palm with the so-called Queen Anne, and quite as quaint and picturesque as the lately revived Tudor styles. Mr. Eastlake called the Tudor styles, by-the-way, or perhaps rather the Elizabethan variety of them, "a miserable compromise by which classic details of the clumsiest description were grafted on buildings supported by the Tudor arch and crowned with the Tudor gable. It is," he continued, "perhaps the bizarre and picturesque character of this bastard style which still renders it popular with the uneducated. To this day Elizabethan mansions are admired by sentimental young ladies." But there are other judges who consider the Tudor styles, and the Elizabethan variety of them, as among

Eastlake Dining-table.

the glories of old England. In the same way condemnation was pronounced upon many matters; among the rest upon all realistic wood-carving; yet the world will always recognize the marvellous beauty of the realistic carving of the Quattrocento, nor will the exquisite work of Grinling Gibbons be ignored, if not in the noblest school of art, nor the charm of the Palissy-ware with its realistic shells, its butterflies and flowers and reptiles. It is scarcely by wholesale condemnations or arbitrary pronunciamentos that real improvement can be made in the direction of art or anything else. The wise seeker is seldom so entirely sure of his attainment as to be absolutely without doubt that another may not be right.

Mr. Eastlake was not always perfectly precise in his archæological information. In commenting, for instance, upon the usual modern dining-table, and with much justice finding it unsatisfactory, he went on to praise an ancient table, and to say that "it was from no lack of skill that this old table was not made capable of being enlarged at pleasure. The social customs of the age in which it was produced did not require such a piece of mechanism. In those days the dining-table was of one uniform length, whether a few or many guests were assembled at it; and I am not sure whether, of the two fashions, the more ancient one does not indicate a more frequent and open hospitality. But be that as it may, if the Jacobean table had been required for occasional extension, we may be certain it would have been so constructed, and that, too, on a more workman-like principle than our foolish telescope slide." But, as a matter of fact, the reader will find in Sir Samuel Myrick's book of ancient specimens, still in preservation, an old table made to pull apart, with a slide and an extension, precisely the thing whose existence is thus denied. In another place, speaking of the design of a piece of Moorish pottery, Mr. Eastlake said : "In the centre or hollow portion is painted, on a white ground and in various colors, a very remarkable pattern. The idea seems to have been taken from a ship, for there are masts and sails, and pennants flying, and port-holes, and a patch of bluish-green below, which, I presume, must be accepted as typical of water. But in such a hurry has the artist been to make his dish gay with color and a pleasant flow of lines, that no one can say which is the bow and which the stern of his vessel, whether we are looking at her athwart or alongships, where the sea ends and the ship's side begins, and finally, what relation the improbable hulk bears to the impossible rigging. The whole thing is, pictorially considered, absolute nonsense, and yet, as a bit of decorative painting, excellent." Now, it is much more likely that, whether the Moorish artist was in a hurry or not to "make his dish gay with color and a pleasant flow of lines," it is not because of that hurry that one cannot say which is the bow and which the stern of his vessel, or where the sea ends and the ship begins, but because of the fact that the Moorish artist was not allowed by the strict requirements of his religion to represent a single article of still or animated life; and desiring to paint the beauty of a ship, he subtly and skilfully represented all the lovely light lines and curves and colors, and suggested all the idea without touching the reality of the airy architecture of the sea.

But these are things apart. And we must confess that it would be hard, on any of the principles of taste that are generally thought sound, to find fault with the greater part of Mr. Eastlake's recommendations, founded as they are upon simplicity, honesty, and propriety. These are the fundamental principles of the Eastlake style, and those on whose basis the upholsterers had to work when the style was demanded; and if artistic taste and grace could be added to them, the style would be perfect. The articles given in Mr. Eastlake's own design were very few, although most of them were fine. There were some chairs, at once exceedingly handsome, stately, and graceful, not at all like the little Eastlake chair most commonly seen; a bedstead and tester, quaint and charming; a hall and extension table; a sideboard, bookcase, and wash-stand; but out of the material of these articles and the hints they afforded, the upholsterers had to provide the whole train of household furniture "after East-

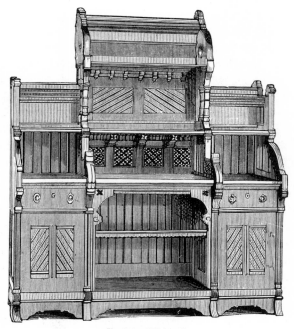

Eastlake Sideboard.

lake." They have succeeded in producing an interesting variety, quaint, with an attractive air of antiquity, full of character and picturesqueness, but always a little stiff, and seldom very graceful. The upholsterers themselves have no fancy for its straight up-and-down angularity; they say they would as lief be shut up all night in a church as in a room with it; and they describe a house furnished in it as seeming too solemn for any of the trivialities of daily life; but if people want it, they must have it. Although they manufacture the article, they still seem to dislike calling it "the Eastlake;" and with some reason, as it so nearly fulfils the requirements of the mediæval as scarcely to need a separate name—not of the lovely pointed Gothic, indeed, with its perpetual poetry and beauty, but of the modernized Gothic, in which the principles of early manufacture are recognized, and whose less striking shapes are better suited to common domestic use. Mr. Eastlake himself made the production of the articles called by his name easy to the furniture-makers. "Every article of furniture," he said, "which is capable of decorative treatment should indicate by its general design the purpose to which it will be applied, and should never be allowed to convey a false notion of that purpose. Experience has shown that particular shapes and special modes of decoration are best suited to certain materials. Therefore the character, situation, and extent of ornament should depend on the nature of the material employed, as well as on the use of the article itself. On the acceptance of these two leading principles — now universally recognized in the field of decorative art—must always depend the chief merit of good design. To the partial and often direct violation of those principles we may attribute the vulgarity and bad taste of most modern work." Farther on Mr. Eastlake added: "The best and most picturesque furniture of all ages has been simple in general form. It may have been enriched by complex details of carved work or inlay, but its main outline was always chaste and sober in design, never running into extravagant contour or unnecessary curves."

Among the decided principles that Mr. Eastlake pronounced for direction are such as that mouldings should be carved from the solid, not made of detached slips of wood glued on a surface; that doors should be hung on long, ornamented, noble hinges; that surfaces should be left in their native hue, never varnished, but if painted at all, painted in flatted color, with a "line introduced here and there to define the construction, with an angle ornament (which may be stencilled) at the corners;" that mitred joints shall be abolished; that joints, moreover, shall be tenoned and pinned together without the nails and glues in use at present; that an article meant to bear weight shall look capable of bearing it; that chests of drawers, and pieces of that sort, shall never bulge out in front, after the style that came in with the Rococo, but shall present a straight line; that curves shall be forsaken, and rounded corners abominated.

The tendency of the present age of upholstery, Mr. Eastlake asserted, is to run into curves—a vicious reminder of the old Louis Quatorze extravagance of contour. "Chairs are invariably curved in such a manner as to insure the greatest amount of ugliness with the least possible comfort. The backs of sideboards are curved in the most senseless and extravagant manner; the legs of cabinets are curved, and become in consequence constructively weak; drawing-room tables are curved in every direction— perpendicularly and horizontally—and are therefore inconvenient to sit at, and always rickety. In marble wash-stands the useful shelf, which should run the whole length of the rear, is frequently omitted in order to insure a curve. This detestable system of ornamentation is called shaping."

Under stress of such remark and instruction, the curve, as usually seen, is not to be found in the Eastlake sofa and chair—the curve rising and sinking on the outlines of the back, and sprawling in and out in those of the legs. The legs and backs of these articles are upright and downright, mortised and tenoned, and connected with under-bars, and consequently rather heavy, and certainly very stiff; and the frame-work of the construction is concealed no more than is inevitable by the springs, padding, and covering. It is not, however, the curve as a line that is objected to, but as a weakener of the fibre of the wood. As a line and an ornament,

Eastlake Chair.

it is frequently to be found in the style — between the shelves of the cabinet, in the round-topped panels of other articles, in many various uses, and in the delicate turner's-work which adorns the backs and arms of chairs, the rolls now and then on the foot-board and head-board of bedsteads, and the posts of dressing-glasses.

Thus it will be seen that the construction to be recognized in the Eastlake style is from the solid wood, unvarnished, usually without veneer, made in the simplest manner that conforms to the purpose of the article, with plain uprights and transverses slightly chamfered at the corners (that is, with a little groove or a narrow slanting slice pared off); and this purpose is always to be declared — there is to be no disposing of a bed by day in the wardrobe or the lounge-box: the bed is a bed, and the wardrobe a wardrobe unmistakably.

Wherever there is a plain surface of wood, as on table-top, sideboard door, or foot-board, if it is not covered with the single deeply moulded panel, or with a multitude of little square panels, it is apt to be made of narrow pieces of wood, laid crosswise, meeting each other pyramidally at one end and retreating at the other, held in place by vertical and horizontal pieces, sometimes the narrow pieces running in one slant all the way, but boxed in after the same fashion.

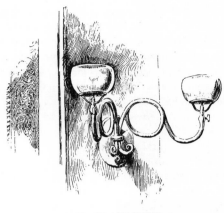

SKETCH FOR A GAS BRACKET.

The Furniture
of
H.H. Richardson

Museum of Fine Arts, Boston

SKETCH FOR AN ANDIRON.

SKETCH FOR CHAIR IN CAPITOL, ALBANY.

HEN Lewis Mumford warned in 1931 that much of the finest design of the "Brown Decades" had already been destroyed, he could hardly have predicted such disasters as the destruction of ten Henry Hobson Richardson buildings in the following thirty years. A tragedy equally great is that, until recently, few of Richardson's admirers have been cognizant that he and his office produced a considerable body of furniture designs, and that these "golden oak horrors" have been totally ignored since Mrs. van Rensselaer's book of 1888. Actually Richardson's furniture is of great originality, and its design, like that of his balustrades, grilles, ironwork, and wall patterns, was thoroughly integrated both in scale and character with his architectural commissions.

Much of Richardson's furniture was integral with the interior woodwork of the buildings and included stair hall and inglenook benches in his houses, and seats, bookcases, and other appurtenances in his libraries, railroad stations, churches and other public buildings. Among the earliest examples of free-standing furniture are the gothic cathedras from the Unity Church in Springfield (1866-69), which were followed by a variety of geometric, leaf-carved and gothic-inspired furniture for Trinity Church (1872-77). The range from the simple, massive forms of the church furniture to the curvaceous arms of the Malden reading room chair of 1885 in so short a span of years is as remarkable as were the variant architectural solutions in the same period. The application of the popular term "Richardson Romanesque" to the furniture can hardly be substantiated, since only a few pieces stem from medieval syntheses and little enough is carved with the leafage familiar in his so-called "Romanesque" buildings. The Woburn Library armchairs (1878) are indeed of early medieval inspiration, but the turned-spindle

Armchair, Woburn Public Library (1878)   *Sidechair, Woburn and North Easton Libraries*

Sidechair, Malden Public Library (1885)

Chair from a photograph in Richardson's office album

Cathedra, Unity Church, Springfield (1869)

chairs of Malden (1885) and Quincy (1880) are related to contemporary works like those of William Morris, and the arm and side chairs of the Malden reading room exhibit early Art Nouveau tendencies.

The furniture drawings preserved in the Richardson Collection at Houghton Library add considerably to our picture of such buildings as the State Capitol at Albany, for which there exist designs for two types of Senate chairs, a Senate desk, and a clock in the Court of Appeals. There are drawings for the original altar table, cathedra, apse chairs and other details of Trinity Church, removed in 1938, and while much of the furniture of the library at Burlington has vanished, a series of seven drawings shows us the spindel-backed benches and chairs with a variety of tables. In a few cases, such as the andirons for Austin Hall (1881) and a spindle armchair and six-legged table for the Malden Library, both the drawings and the objects themselves have survived.

Other furniture is known only through photographic records, such as a sidechair with cartwheel arms, related to the Woburn Library reading room benches. This may have been designed for private use, like another chair in a drawing labelled "for Olly Ames — 1 doz Chairs to be of St. Domingo Mahogany." While little of this residential furniture has been discovered, there are a sofa, a chair and a dressing table which Richardson designed for his own home, and an inglenook bench of elaborate dimensions and a porch bench designed for the Ames Gate Lodge at North Easton.

The variety seen in the existing examples, the drawings and photographs reveal the sanity, power and urbanity of the designs, and place Richardson among the masters of 19th century furniture design.

Richard H. Randall, Jr.

Reading room bench, Woburn Public Library (1878)   courtesy the author and publisher

BOOK-CASE

Russell Lynes

Palace exposition in London in 1851 and the Paris Exposition of 1867 had brought together the artistic outpourings and crafts of strange lands and had opened the eyes of Americans who had visited them to all sorts of undreamed-of decorations for the home—Persian carpets and brass samovars and Moorish furniture inlaid with mother of pearl. All these were combined with the elaborately ornamented rosewood chairs and tables and sofas turned out by furniture factories, with mirrors in gilded scroll-saw frames, and whatnots aching with bibelots. "It has become proverbial among European manufacturers," wrote an architect in the seventies who was determined to bring order out of chaos, "that whatever is so wanting in good taste as to ruin it for the home market, will do for the United States.

No one had added a dash of fresh spice to the aesthetic arguments about how people should live since Downing's death, and he would have been the first to admit that his words had grown dim in the public ears. After a long period of extremely tasty debauchery, there were many Americans ready to hit the sawdust trail to salvation, and Charles L. Eastlake, the new messiah, was on hand to help them.

"Suddenly the voice of the prophet Eastlake was heard crying in the wilderness," *Harper's Bazar* reported. " 'Repent ye, for the Kingdom of the Tasteful is at hand!' "

Actually Eastlake spoke in a rather quiet voice and he was directing his sermon on taste to his compatriots in England and not to Americans at all. The effect of his words, however, was almost equally magical on both sides of the Atlantic. No prophet of taste in our era has ever precipitated such a pell-mell revolution with such a slim volume as did Eastlake with his *Hints on Household Taste*. It was published first in this country in 1872, three years after it was issued in England, and immediately became the manifesto and the testament and the book of revelations, all in one. Households were completely refurbished to follow its teachings; furniture manufacturers and upholsterers were forced to scrap their old designs and patterns to follow its dicta; young brides declined to set up housekeeping with anything that it did not certify as "artistic."

If the furniture and the aesthetic trappings that Eastlake so persuasively recommended seem to us now as cumbersome as anything that the nineteenth century produced, we must remember that to our grandparents not only had they the fascination of a new look, but that the arguments that went with them had the ring of high moral purpose and high aesthetic ideals. Here was a chance not only to redecorate but to be saved at the same time.

Like Downing, Eastlake was concerned not only with aesthetics but with morals, though he faced them aggressively rather than with Downing's gentleness. He was disgusted with the low state to which taste had fallen, and with the way in which the public invariably seemed to scamper off in pursuit of the latest fad, no matter how silly or extravagant or capricious. He was especially hostile to everything he considered to be sham and showy rather than, to use his favorite word, "sincere," and he blamed the intolerable situation about equally on women and on shopkeepers. It was not that he failed to understand the fickleness of taste, but he could not condone it. "This absurd love of change—simply for the sake of change," he wrote, "is carried to such an extent that if one desires to replace a jug or a table cloth with another of the same pattern, even a few months after it was first bought, however good the style may have been, it is extremely difficult, sometimes impossible to do so. The answer is always the same. 'Last year's goods, sir. We couldn't match them now.'" He blamed the purchasers and not the manufacturers. "So long as a thirst for mere novelty exists independently of all artistic considerations, the aim at Manchester and Sheffield will be to produce objects which, by their singular form or striking combination of colors, shall always appear new."

This kind of impatience with novelty-seeking and the tone of Eastlake's attack sound almost monotonously familiar to us today. We have been continually exposed to the entreaties and attacks of critics, designers, and promoters of modern houses and furniture who have tried to make us lead more reasonable lives in more "functional" surroundings. But to Eastlake's contemporaries this was a new note, a clarion call. The very notion that simplicity of design and "sincerity" of construction should be identified with good taste was an astonishing reversal of Victorian notions of luxury and comfort. And that good taste could also be inexpensively come by was nearly revolutionary. "Excellence of design," Eastlake pronounced, "may be, and, indeed, frequently is, quite independent of cost. . . . Some of the worst specimens of decorative art that I see exposed for sale are expensive articles of luxury. Some of the most appropriately formed, and therefore most artistic, objects of household use are to be bought for a trifling sum."

Eastlake's ideas of "functionalism," though that word was not to come into the language of design until about half a century later, took something from Ruskin, who believed that "the essential and necessary structure of an object should never be lost sight of nor concealed by secondary forms or ornament" and something from William Morris and his handicraft movement. Eastlake had no patience with unnecessary curves, so essential a part of the furniture designed in the "French taste," because they seemed to deny the essential function of a piece of furniture, which should be strong of construction, forthright in its purpose, and, above all, comfortable. A chair or table or even a mantelpiece to be sincere should be put together with wooden pegs and dowels and not with nails and screws. A wooden peg had "sincerity," a nail did not. "I do not exactly see," he wrote, "how veneering is to be rejected on 'moral' grounds," but he disliked it because it was used to cover shoddy cabinetwork and because it was inclined to blister.

It is not difficult to see why such sensible ideas, which combined moral uplift, high aesthetic ideals, practicality, and physical comfort, should have delighted so many. Nor is it difficult to understand why so many writers and other promoters of the public taste should have rallied to make Eastlake a household word and something of a household deity. This was the tidiest parcel of taste anyone had seen in a long while—a veritable C-ration for the sensibilities. Eastlake had not only offered a new look, but he had given a complete set of practical instructions for putting it into effect. More important than this he had also provided a neat and easily mastered set of arguments that any housewife could learn and recite with conviction. This was packaged aesthetics for everyday use. The catch phrases—"sincerity," "picturesqueness," "the quaint," and "the artistic"—became part of every woman's vocabulary and (think how Eastlake would have disliked it). Under pressure from the considerable numbers who demanded "Eastlake furniture," manufacturers (who had no love for Eastlake because of what he had written about the shoddy work they turned out) began to run up tables and chairs and bookcases and cupboards that were a parody of what Eastlake had in mind but which at the same time had an undeniable affinity to his own pieces. They were angular and bulky, and about as close to Eastlake in spirit as the overstuffed modern of today is to the early designs of the Bauhaus.

FIRE PLACE IN FARM HOUSE WEST HARTFORD CONNECTICUT

THE ILLUSTRATED

WOOD WORKER

FOR JOINERS — CABINET MAKERS — STAIR BUILDERS — CARPENTERS — CAR BUILDERS — &c. &c.

VOL. 1   No. 6   JUNE, 1879.   PRICE TEN CENTS.

Bookcase · Designed · By · F. W. Angell · Prov. R.I.

THE ILLUSTRATED WOOD WORKER

FOR JOINERS · CABINET MAKERS · STAIR BUILDERS · CARPENTERS · CAR BUILDERS. &c. &c

VOL. 1   No. 7.   JULY, 1879.   PRICE TEN CENTS.

GENT'S · TOILET · STAND

BOOK-CASE AND WRITING-TABLE COMBINED.

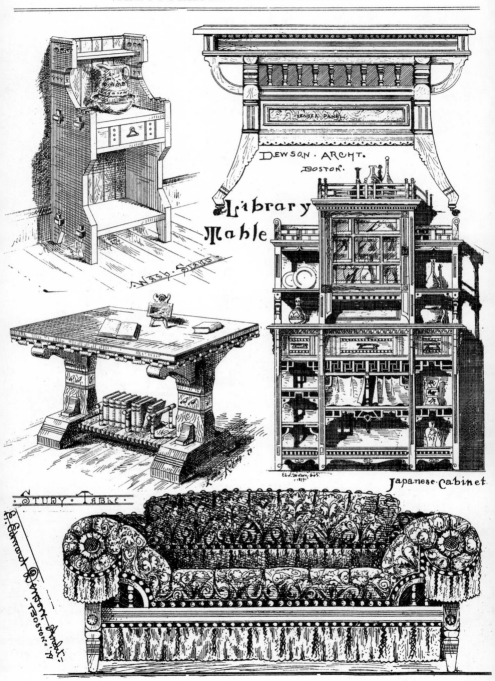

Wash-Stand

DEWSON. ARCHT.
BOSTON.

Library Table

Study Table

Japanese Cabinet

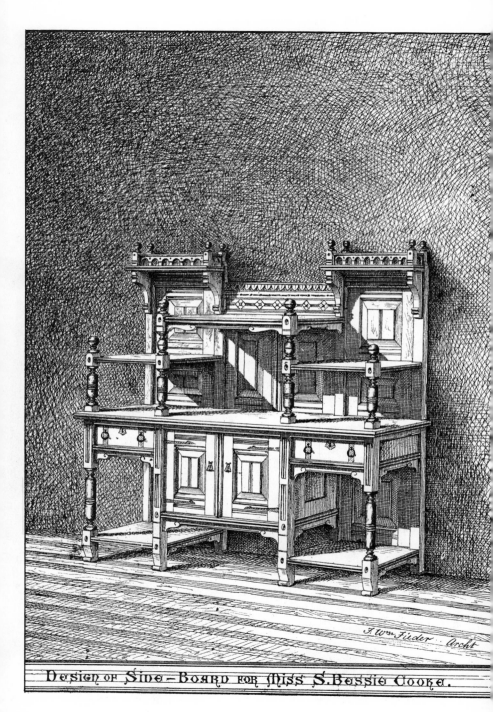

DESIGN OF SIDE-BOARD FOR MISS S. BESSIE COOKE.

F. Wm. Fieder. Archt

INDEX

Apostle spoons, 110-1
Architectural styles, 89
Art furniture, 45
Art in Common Objects, 114-6
Axminster carpets, 51
Barry, 18
Bed-curtains, 94-6
Bedrooms, 31, 175-90
Bedstead (Eastlake design), 90, 92-4
Book case (Eastlake design), 58
Bookcases, 147-8
Brussels carpets, 51, 56
Candlesticks, 70-2
Carpets, 12-13, 47-51, 97, 133-4
Carved furniture, 27-8
Chairs, Dining-room, 41-4
Chairs, Drawing-room, 82
Cheffonier, 64
Chests of Drawers, 98-9
Chevreul, 60
Clothing, 8, 105-7
Color for furniture, 59-61
Costume, 105-7
Crinoline, 106-7
Crockery, 100-1
Crystal Palace Exhibition (1851), 30, 107
Curves in furniture, 25
Decorations of walls, 85-7
Dining a'la Russe, 14-15
Dining-rooms, 31, 151-74
Dining Tables, 169-74
Door moldings, 57
Drawing-rooms, 31, 33
Eastlake Furniture, 163-8, 182, 199-204
Elegance, False notions of, 75
Embroidery, 14
Entrance halls, 31-3, 125-130
Epergnes, 108
Etagere, Chinese, 143-4, 174
Floor coverings, 20-1
French polishing, 40-1
Functionalism in furniture design, 45
Furniture, cost of well-designed, 81-2
Furniture, Good design in, 75-80
Furniture ornament, 82-4
Gas lighting, 160-03
Glass ware, 102-4

Glastonbury chairs, 33
Gothic Revival, 16-19
Hats, 106
Iron work, 63-65-7
Kidderminster carpets, 51
Knives and forks, 113
Lighting fixtures, 68-70, 160-3
Landseer, 14
Living-rooms, 131-50
Majolica, 100
Mantel-piece (Eastlake design), 61-3
Massive furniture, 163
Milliners, 10-11
Minton, 20
Morris & Co., 134
New York Town Houses, 125-30
Novelties, Demand for, 13-14
Oak, Foolish practice of varnishing new, 56-7
Ornament, Nature of, 45
Parliament, House of, 18
Parquetry Floors, 48, 50
Pianos, 149-50
Picturesque furniture, 75
Plumbing and heating, 185-6
Pugin, 17-19, 88
Puritan Furniture, 168
Ruskin, 88
Scott, Walter, 17
Scroll work, 27-8
Settle, A., 138
Sideboards, 46, 167
Silver holloware, 111
Silverplated wares, Color in, 109
Silver-plating, 26
Silverware patterns, 109-11
Sofas and Chairs, 135-41
Tables, 34-9, 140-3, 156-9
Table-settings, Dinner, 108
Taste, Acquirement of, 9-10
Tea and Coffee Urns, 67-9
Tiles, Eucaustic, 20, 22, 24
Toilet-tables, 97-8
Turkey Carpets, 51, 56
Varnishing furniture, 40-1, 56-7, 102
Veneering, 25-7
Wall coverings, 21-3, 53-5
Wall-furniture, 85-7
Walpole, Horace, 17
Windsor chair, 28-9, 100

Hanging Shelves.

Picture Frame

Plain Bracket

-·Study·for·a·Chair·-

STUDIES FOR AMATEURS.